CW00547467

Wine

This is a Parragon Book

This edition published in 2003

Parragon

Queen Street House

4 Queen Street

Bath BA1 1HE, UK

Copyright © Parragon 2001

ISBN: 1-40540-275-X

A copy of the CIP data for this book is available from the British Library upon request.

The right of Mick Middles to be identified as the author of this work has been asserted in accordance with Section 77 of the Copyright, Designs and Patents Act of 1988.

Editorial, design and layout by Essential Books

Printed and bound in China

Wine

Mick Middles

CONTENTS

Introduction

The Wine Revolution

'...and you go and choose the wine!'

This used to be a simple request. Back in, say, the 1970s, it would, more often than not, be delivered by a wife to her dutiful husband, who would merrily skip along to the supermarket's wine section, while the wife would busy herself in the rather more complex world of, well, burgers or something equally undemanding.

The husband didn't mind. He enjoyed this bit. It was easy. They could have white, red or rosé. Yes, he would linger awhile, glancing over the 'posh bottles' from France. There might be twenty of these. Mouton Rothschild. He liked the sound of that. It sounded kind of 'classy'. He wouldn't buy it. Too expensive and way out of his league. But he liked looking at it and the other French wines. There would be 'Mouton Cadet' and something called 'Beaujolais'. There would be a few dusty bottles, with fading labels which proclaimed Château this or Château that. It didn't matter what they actually said, or what was in the bottle. If it was a special occasion, he would buy one. That would be it. He would buy a bottle of French red wine. That would be classy enough. That was all anyone needed to know. He might buy a white. He might, if the occasion demanded, buy a Sauternes. He wasn't sure exactly what that was. It tasted a bit sweet to him, but what did it matter? It was only wine. For very, very special occasions, he might even plumb for a bottle of Moët and Chandon. They'd had that at that restaurant, once. Great it was. Got rid of all that sauce that they had smeared across his steak.

But mostly, he wouldn't need to bother with anything so complicated. Mostly it would be a simple choice. Probably the Mateus Rosé. Everyone liked that. Possibly the Thunderbird. That was good. Always got him drunk. It really matter didn't matter. It was just wine.

There is a part of me, I fully admit, that longs for such simplicity. It's not that the fantastic world of wine that has engulfed us all, or at least most of us, bringing with it a whole universe of complex and exotic tastes, is a bad thing. It's not. It simply wonderful and, once we entered into it, we could never, ever go back. But, well, as we washed down our Prawn Cocktails with our Liebfraumilch, or our tacos with our Thunderbird, we

Introduction

didn't know any better, did we? We were blissful in our ignorance. It was a simple life. Wine was wine. It tasted like ... wine. It didn't taste like '...the inside of an old lady's purse, topped by a hint of mint and spicy overtones which fade to a crisp finish of fresh cut grass...' Such an idea would have seemed absurd.

Today the 'You go and choose the wine' request doesn't necessarily seem so innocent. You might have friends over, friends who always seem so knowledgeable on the subject of wine. Those friends who definitely turned their noses up at that bottle of Bulgarian red you took to their dinner party. True, it did seem a little bit musty and perhaps you should have splashed out more. But where has this idea that everyone has to be a wine expert come from?

Well, the simple answer is that, you don't. You don't have to have extensive knowledge of French appellations. You don't even have to know what an appellation is. But a grasp of the mere basics is a wonderful thing. It will carry you beyond the borders that keep you locked in the 'Do you want red, white or rosé?' world. It will introduce you to a new world that is complex, deeply fascinating and, most of all, great fun. You don't have to become a wine snob, although that probably will start to happen. (Before long you may find yourself coming away from a dinner party, saying words like, 'Nice couple ... can't believe they served that Lambrusco Bianco though...') Don't worry. Don't take it too seriously. It happens to everybody.

A little wine knowledge will stop *you* from being that couple who served that Lambrusco Bianco. More importantly than that, it will prevent you from feeling that sense of terror as you enter into the vast, dizzying, confusing, mind-boggling expanse of the wine department at your local supermarket. That moment when hundreds of bottles are screaming at you from the shelves, gimmicky and trendy looking labels tempting you as you trundle past, hoping beyond hope that the bottle you eventually 'panic buy' will not prove to be too embarrassing.

It's easier than you think. Just a little knowledge will carry you beyond the horror you feel when you glance at the labels and notice words like 'Zinfandel', 'Pinot Noir' and 'Sauvignon Blanc'. I do know people, extremely intelligent people with high-flying jobs as it happens, who spent years buying wines without knowing that such words were actually grape varieties. Perhaps it didn't matter, if they enjoyed the wines anyway. But just a tiny amount of information about the basic properties of each grape will unlock another door and make your trip around those supermarket shelves that bit more interesting.

Selecting wine is easy. You look at the country of origin; look at the producer; look at the label name; look at the grape; look at the price. Already you have all the information you need. If the wine is particularly enjoyable, or disappointingly dull, make a mental note – or jot down a couple of lines to remind yourself – and move on to your next shopping trip. Almost immediately this becomes fun. An adventure. Certainly more fun than deciding which dog food to buy.

This little book is simply an aid to helping you to move along that route. It will not turn you into a wine bore. I promise you that much.

During the past ten years, a wine revolution has taken place on a global scale. It is a question of good marketing, rampant commercialism and improving logistics and distribution. It is also a market response to the increasing demands of consumers who are, in general, becoming more and more knowledgeable and more and more demanding. Nothing wrong with that. There is much good news. Despite resistance from some of the traditional wine producers – and, even in France, this tide has now turned – the wine industry has been quick to adapt to new wine-making techniques. Although there are situations where new wines have been 'drummed up' by the scientists, nobody can deny that the general standard of wine has risen tremendously during the past ten years, and continues to rise.

The chances of buying a 'bad' bottle are now lower than ever. But, most astonishing of all, is that revolution in logistics. If you stand up, right now, walk out the door and go to your local corner shop, you may well find a bottle of good quality wine from some small wine producer in, say, Chile, and it may well be priced below the cost of a single takeaway meal. This is something that I find absolutely extraordinary and I make no apologies for repeating it later on in this book. The world of wine is at your fingertips. (Quite literally, if you order via the Internet.)

This book is a basic guide. If there is a central rule, then it may tempt you to stretch from the low to the mid-price bracket, where an amazing variety of quality wines await. It's not a hard and fast rule. There are many good wines below this bracket and, conversely, some producers have unfortunately cottoned on to the fact that sales can

Introduction

actually improve by hoiking the price of a wine, packaging it elegantly and casting a general impression of quality. Of course that happens, but it is still the exception. I have yet to meet a single person who has bought a disappointing bottle of, say, Wolf Blass from South Australia, or Fetzer from California.

The revolution is upon us. It can seem daunting. It can seem absurd. This is because, by and large, it is, indeed, absurd. But that's all part of the wonderful enigma of wine.

THE WORLD OF WINE

The notion that the world of wine is a surreal place, completely separated from reality as you and I know it, is highlighted by the language of wine and by the myths that surround the tasting, buying and storing of wine. Here's a brief introduction to the wonderful world of wine.

Tasting Terms

Within the wine world, words seem to change their meaning. There are terms used in wine-tasting that you will not encounter anywhere else on earth.

Some of them have meanings that are, I admit, obvious. Others vary from the mildly absurd to the plain stupid. Some of them are used in this book. Many aren't. All of them, however ludicrous they may seem, are quite fun when you get to know them.

Here is a short glossary of the main wine-tasting terms.

Aftertaste: In the world of food, particularly fish, an aftertaste is generally a bad thing. In wine it is all-important. It is the most reliable indicator of the quality of the wine. The length of the aftertaste, which varies tremendously, is often called 'the finish'.

Aroma: There's nothing weird about this one. We all know that wines can have strong and distinctive smells. However, it is not an indicator of quality. Some good wines have pungent aromas and some lovely, fresh smelling wines can taste like battery acid (see England).

Balance: The wine's components – fruitiness, dryness/sweetness, acidity, tannin, strength, etc. – form the balance. A well-balanced wine will see all components working in harmony.

Bouquet: The bouquet is not quite the same as the aroma. It is usually reserved for wines of greater quality.

Complex: There are many mentions, in this little book, of the 'complex' nature of wine. You may well ask, 'How can a wine be complex?' It is a good question. But complexity is the most important aspect of a wine. It can only be achieved when the many flavours are balanced in a way that allows them all to come through in the taste. A wine that lacks complexity is often dominated by one central flavour. A more complex wine will allow flavours to complement each other, change and linger in the length. The great beauty of wine is its ability to 'throw in' unexpected and unusual flavours. Often they just flicker briefly. Non wine lovers may scoff, when it is

Tasting Terms

mentioned that a wine has '..a hint of nettles' or 'dark brown chocolate with hints of vanilla', but the fact is that wine is something that can hold a wild and sometimes fairly bizarre range of tastes.

Corked: If a wine is said to be 'corked' it doesn't mean there are bits of corked floating around. (That just means you have a lousy wine waiter). It means the wine has been affected by mould on the cork. A good indication is a musty, damp cardboard or wet leathery smell. If the taste continues this unpleasantness, the bottle has to go back. Slowly, as we edge further and further into a world of plastic corks, even in France, this problem will be all but eradicated from young wines.

Crisp: White wines in particular are 'crisp' when the acidity is perfectly in balance.

Earthy: A good one, this. Wines often reflect the distinctive type of soil of a particular area. Earthiness is an indicator of the complexity of a wine.

Finish: The pocket of taste that lingers after you have sipped your wine. This can vary in length and is a good indicator of quality.

Hard: A 'hard' wine can be a wine that is too young. It generally refers to too much acidity or a taste that is too 'tannic'. There is no complexity to the wine because of these dominant factors.

Nose: aroma or bouquet.

Powerful: Usually a reference to the alcoholic strength although occasionally used to describe deep rich red wines ... which are often strong but that's not necessarily the reason for the wine's powerful nature.

Steely: Rieslings are often described as 'steely'. It refers to the metallic taste which comes from high acidity. This is not usually a bad thing. Steeliness hints that the high acidity is well-balanced rather than dominant.

Supple: Round, smooth. The opposite of steely. Usually used in reference to reds, but not always.

Sweet: Normally a simple reference to the amount of sugar in the wine, but sometime a 'sweet' wine is a wine with rich or ripe flavourings.

Tough: Well, we have all drunk these, tough red wines that taste like old shoes.

There are many more, but I have tried not to use too many in this little guide.

Ordering Wine

I cannot believe there is a single person reading this who hasn't suffered that embarrassing little ritual which goes with ordering wine in restaurants. After the choosing, tasting and nodding pompously to the wine waiter that it is acceptable to you, comes that little pocket of tension, when you realize that everyone else at your table is now following your lead. What if the wine is too acidic after all? You didn't notice it, you idiot! What if it was just a bad choice and you are going to have spend an extraordinary amount of money on what is little more than dull plonk?

Don't worry. It's not your fault.

Always remember that *you* are the customer. You are the one paying for this. You are not being asked to judge the quality of the wine. The fact is that, after one first sip, you can't really tell anyway. All you are being asked to do is test whether the bottle is drinkable, or whether it tastes like battery acid. Forget everything else.

What's more, and if you are in Britain this is particularly applicable, it is not your fault that restaurant wine prices are quite unacceptably high. There is no reason for this other than the fact that restaurants bang up this price and regard it as 'handling expenses'. Yes, they have to take your order, fumble around the wine rack situated behind the till, open the bottle, put you through the absurd ritual mentioned above and serve it in, hopefully, clean and appropriate glasses.

Unless it is a special occasion, all you really want, when you enter a restaurant, is a tasty, affordable wine that will enhance your meal. There is absolutely nothing wrong with stating this to the wine waiter and hurtling the decision back in his direction. After all, he is paid to know what wines complement which meals in the restaurant.

As a rule, if the restaurant is of reasonable quality, don't start showing off to your new girlfriend, boyfriend or friends by pompously perusing the list and ordering something with a huge price tag that they will loathe. Ask them what kind of wine they like. If you are still stuck, convey this to the wine waiter. Nothing wrong with saying, 'They like a dry white ... what would you suggest?'

Personally I tend to save my wine exploration for the home and, at a restaurant, opt for the 'house' wine. You are still fully entitled to complain if it is not up to scratch. After all, the house wine has been chosen as a result of *their* professional expertise. It is an important indicator of the quality of *their* restaurant.

Buying Wine

Where Do I Buy My Wine?

This is one of those questions that is made far more complicated and irritating than it needs to be. The fact is, it doesn't matter. The selection of wines now on offer at any supermarket is quite fantastic. What's more, it changes all the time, keeping pace with shifts, trends and even new countries. If your wine knowledge is not too clever, this is your perfect learning ground, as wine from across the board, at all prices and all countries will be on display. You will not be able to glean too much information from the spotty shelf-stacker you find lurking in the Australian section, but it doesn't really matter.

If you wish to take it a stage further, there is a list of more specialist wine stockists and importers further on in this book. You could do far worse than opt for an Oddbins. The staff there will certainly be knowledgeable and helpful. Again, don't be embarrassed to ask any questions at all. Remember, you are the customer and they are the experts. Let them guide you.

If there is a local specialized wine stockist, who runs a

wine club, then you really are in luck. Join the club, get to know the stockist and go to the local wine tastings. The chances are that he, she or they will have built up their business from sheer enthusiasm. Furthermore, as the competition is absolutely ferocious, it is wholly in their interests to offer a more personal service.

In my experience, wine stockists are only too pleased to tell you of their buying exploits and they will litter their tales with examples of the better wines they have brought back. This is important. Such knowledge really does tend to enhance the curiosity value of a bottle of wine. I recall one such small operator, who sent out mail shots detailing his European adventures. The effect it had was stunning. It simply made you want to try the wines ... it added a certain colour. It was also great fun. You felt you were sharing something.

Open any Sunday newspaper supplement these days, and the chances are that you will encounter an advertisement asking for your credit card number and promising to send you a case of specially selected wines. There is nothing wrong with these offers and, generally speaking, they provide good wines at an extremely reasonable cost. Whether this is a good option or not,

Buying Wine

depends on you. Having a case arrive that has been selected for you by a computer operator can take away a bit of the fun. On the other hand, you may well have no time to choose yourself and feel the service is worthwhile. It's just a simple choice. There are no rules.

And finally, many people ask whether or not they should take the slightest bit of notice of those ludicrous folk who champion wine on the hundreds of food and drink television programmes that cluster together on the television schedules. Again the answer is perfectly simple. Accept them for the entertainment they are. They have played a large part in alerting us all to the wine revolution in recent years. They have also built very lucrative careers out of exploiting the mystery and enigma of wine. Well, good for them. They certainly have added to the fun. They are not to be taken too seriously although they are, almost always, knowledgeable and fired by genuine enthusiasm. They do no harm.

Good Years, Bad Years

The world of 'vintage' wine is not something that is covered in this book. This is partly because it is intended as an introduction to wine that deals with the incredible number of new and very good wines that are now available to everyone at reasonable prices, and also because the very notion of selecting a 'good vintage' seems almost absurd these days. Although, even now, there are good years and bad years in most wine-producing regions in the world, modern wine-making techniques have caused the difference between the two to be minimal, to say the least.

It wasn't always so. In vast wine-making countries, France in particular, the quality of the wine was dependent on the grape harvest. This would vary year by year, depending on the weather and soil quality. The best wines would be laid down in cellars and the mystique of particular wine years would be allowed to grow.

Today, the idea of storing wine does not carry the same level of mystique. (Unless you are a serious wine collector, and if you are then it is highly unlikely that you will be reading this.) As I've said, the vast majority of good wines of today are ready to be drunk straight away. It might also be

Good Years, Bad Years

noted that, contrary to popular belief, wine does not necessarily improve with age. Not even red wine. There are those who believe that the old notions of wine improving with age still apply to French wines, particularly from Bordeaux. Not so.

What happens to a wine that is allowed to age is interesting. It will lose its primary flavours. That lovely sharp fruitiness that is characteristic of so much wine today will fade in time spent in the bottle and softer flavours, dried fruits, earthiness, leathery smoky textures, will come to the fore. Is this a good thing? Well, it can give the wine a more sophisticated taste. The wine could be more mellow than it was, say, ten years previously. Is it worth it? Maybe, but remember, wine can also worsen with age to the point that it becomes completely undrinkable.

It's true, some wine does improve with age, but this is a complex area best left to the experts. Most good wine merchants or warehouses will have staff who will be able to tell you what wines are particularly suited to the ageing process. In brief, most Riesling will age well. Australian Shiraz is apparently another good bet as well as a good many wines from Languedoc or the Douro valley.

GRAPES

What makes wines taste different? Well, the most important factor is the choice of grape used to make them. Learn to recognize the different grape varieties and you're on the road to becoming a wine expert.

The Main Grapes

Reds

Cabernet Franc

A bit of a challenge, this one. The rest of the world has looked upon this rather second-rate French and Italian grape with a certain amount of distrust. Generally speaking, Cabernet Franc is a table wine grape. It has no genuine depth and, for this reason, people who have a headache waiting for the merest sip of a rich red, tend to place their trust in Cabernet Franc.

However, certain vineyards in the Loire Valley have proved that Cabernet Franc can produce a disarmingly powerful wine from this most curious grape. As such, one senses that a small cult following has started to grow. Who knows, wine bar superstardom may beckon. Australians, New Zealanders, South Africans and Californians have chosen to largely ignore it. At their peril? Well, anything is possible.

Cabernet Sauvignon

The greatest red of all? Probably. It is a grape of many talents and seems to be loved by wine buffs, weekend guzzlers and that strange dwindling breed who only partake at Christmas and on birthdays, thus depriving themselves of year-round pleasure. Whether they all know it or not, one thing is certain. If they have enjoyed red wine, then they have enjoyed the rich blackcurrant characters of Cabernet Sauvignon. One fact seems to ride above all others. Cabernet Sauvignon forms the bulk of Claret. That alone is enough to give the grape a mythical, untouchable status.

From its French roots, Cabernet Sauvignon has spread successfully around the world, its ability to thrive in different climates and wildly different locations has kept the grape at the heart of the world wine revolution. Most obviously, the Cabernets of Australia, South Africa and California have grasped our attention with that distinctive luxurious fruit at the fore.

Most of us remain fond of that moment, perhaps deep into the heart of a Saturday night, with friends gathered

The Main Grapes

round, when that rich cassis flavour has suddenly kicked in. 'Ooooh...lovely wine...' we say, affecting disturbingly pompous tones. But that's the real beauty of Cabernet Sauvignon. Even when, as is so often the case, it is only one component of a good wine, it still manages to arrest the attention.

In fact, the grape's ability to mingle well with other grapes, is partly the reason for its success. It even creeps into some of the great Australian Shirazes that have crowded our supermarket shelves during the past ten years.

In Bordeaux, the traditional practice has been to mix Cabernet Sauvignon with Merlot, and the plummy character of the latter grape adds a subtlety to Cabernet Sauvignon, producing some of the finest red wines of all time.

Grenache

Grenache used to be the silent grape. Everybody had sampled it but nobody knew it. Nevertheless, it was there, in all the carafes served up in French bistros, or cheap eating holes. Grenache formed the basis of table wine. It was palatable, and improved glass by glass, but there was never any real depth.

The problem with the Grenache grape is that it is easy to grow in large quantities, but the percentage of quality grapes will always be low. Therefore, traditionally, good and bad would be harvested together and used to make that quick, cheap, table wine.

However, given a caring vineyard, a little more expense and time, Grenache can actually hold its own and produce cherry-like wines, with a zing of raspberry and a slight peppery aroma. Curiously, the emergence of quality Grenache owes a great deal to the Australians who nurtured the grape for the middle price range. As such, Grenache has become hugely popular in wine bars and is now beginning to be eagerly sought on the supermarket shelves.

Merlot

Because of that traditional relationship with Cabernet Sauvignon, Merlot used to have the indignity of being regarded as the poorer and duller partner, merely a grape that helped the Cabernet Sauvignon reach greater heights. This was never really the case. Merlot had catalyst qualities and has always been distinctive in its own right.

Any prejudice against Merlot, however, has now all

The Main Grapes

been wiped away. It was certainly one of the trendiest grapes of the 1990s and, unlike a couple of notable whites that enjoyed similar attention, Merlot has never fallen out of fashion.

In Bordeaux, they now plant more Merlot than Cabernet Sauvignon. If used on its own, it often produces a wine with a mixed berry flavour, set off by a slight sweetness which arguably accounts for its popularity. At the top end of the market, some of the glorious classic reds of St Emilion are dominated by the flavours of Merlot.

Away from France, Merlot has not quite matched the success of Cabernet Sauvignon, the main reason being that Australia never linked it with Shiraz. However, in California it has been used to make wines blessed with a richness that hadn't previously been the forte of the American market. It might also be noted that the swell of wine-producing activity in South America – in particular, Chile and, to a lesser extent, Brazil – owes a great deal to the fruitiness of its main grape, Merlot. Unlike in Australia, Merlot does now seem to be thriving in New Zealand as well (the Hawkes Bay region favours this grape).

Nebbiolo

Nebbiolo, probably the most beautifully named grape of all, is the classic Italian red. (The word Nebbiolo may hint at lovely Italianate architecture seen on a sunny day but in fact the word comes from the word *nebbia*, meaning dank, dense fog.) It's a strange one. In young wines it usually disappoints. In fact, the 'laying down' of a Nebbiolo wine is usually recommended, and the longer it lies, the better. (So, it's not really a wine to pluck quickly from the supermarket shelves at 7pm on a Friday night.) However, a mature Nebbiolo wine is usually fascinatingly complex, with the dark, rich, moody taste challenged by a most unlikely perfume.

It is, and will remain, fundamentally Italian. However if, like me, you have spent many Friday nights munching on Mexican food, the chances are you will have used, say, a La Cetto to soften the sting of peppers and salsa. La Cetto, a Mexican wine governed from LA, is as popular as Corona beer in California, and with good reason.

The Main Grapes

Syrah/Shiraz

now, I know, it's confusing. Australians, for reasons that have never been made clear, reinvented the Syrah grape under the name Shiraz. Most people are now well aware of this but there was a hugely embarrassing, and perhaps quite comic, period when wine lovers new to the game would rigorously compare the two. Perhaps the Australians just wanted us to keep a check on our pretensions. So here we have it. Syrah ... Shiraz ... exactly the same grape. Just accept that and move on.

Actually, the two names do help us concentrate on the two major successes scored by this grape. In France it has attained great success in the northern Rhone region, where it rules the roost. It has also sprung up in the South of France, particularly in Languedoc. Just as a measure of its potential, Syrah is the main component in Châteauneuf-du-Pape.

In recent years, it is the Australians who have grasped Shiraz and taken it to a new marketing level. Its taste – dark, solid-bodied, toffee with rich herbs peeking through – is sometimes surprisingly complex, especially for Australian wines that are boldly popularist. There have been times when everyone seemed to be drinking Rosemount Shiraz on

Friday evenings, and why not? The Australian success of Shiraz was kick-started by the glorious wines of the Penfolds Grange. Once they had set the precedent, the rest of Australia joined in, hailing Shiraz the king of Oz grapes.

Tempranillo

The word 'Tinto' often indicates the dominance of Tempranillo in a wine. It is most famous for being the heart of Rioja, where it blends with Garnacha. It can be found in wines throughout Spain and Portugal, where it is also used to make port.

Just to confuse the issue, in the Alentejo region of Portugal they chose to call it Aragonez. Tempranillo wines are usually light in colour and enriched by the strong pull of vanilla.

Zinfandel

For what it's worth, the favoured grape of the writer of this little book. Zinfandel is the grape that breaks the rules. It is the punk grape. Although originally from Italy, it has laid down its roots in California and Mexico where it defies the terrain on which it grows, and exudes hedgerow aromas and a deep rich taste that lies beyond strawberry.

The Main Grapes

Zinfandel is everything that it shouldn't be. And then, just when you think you've got it pinned down, you pluck another bottle from the supermarket shelves and this seems rebelliously unlike all the other Zinfandels you have tasted. This is definitely not a grape to recommend too heartily, for it cannot be trusted. However, you won't go far wrong with anything from the Santa Cruz mountains.

It is occasionally used as a component in oversweet blush wines and one senses that the grape resents that particular usage. But, take my advice, be brave with Zinfandel. Experiment and live dangerously.

Whites

Chardonnay

Poor old Chardonnay! Regarded by many, unfairly as it happens, as the grape of the post-yuppie generation. A grape which flickered brightly for a trendy moment, and then fell from fashion like flares or leg-warmers.

Chardonnay seems to symbolize an endless summer, when everyone appeared to labour under the illusion that if a wine is deep yellow in colour and tasted as if it had been fermented from the sweepings of a carpenter's workshop, then it could be regarded as a drop of quality.

The Californians and the Australians can still be blamed for promoting this simplistic angle. However, blaming the Chardonnay grape for all the overpriced 'oak aged' yellow stuff that flowed so freely in the wine bars of the early 1990s is grossly unfair. Those big, vulgar bosomy 'oak aged' wines are merely one type of Chardonnay. Indeed, far from being one-dimensional, it is arguably the most flexible white grape of them all. Please remember this the next time that someone informs you that they '...no longer drink Chardonnay ... it's Chablis for us these days, a much more refined taste...'. Well, you can agree with them if you wish but I imagine it will be hard not to inform them that, actually, the grapes used to create Chablis are ... yes indeed, Chardonnay grapes!

Bizarrely, the marketing people do seem to have cottoned on to this. If you peruse the supermarket shelves right now, you will find a number of Chardonnays that pleadingly offer the words, 'Not oak aged'. Trust them. For they will lead you into a new age, the age of the born-again Chardonnay. Try Italian Chardonnay, for example, if you are searching for a delicate, elegant white to complement a crisp salad.

The Main Grapes

The true home of Chardonnay is not the sun-kissed surfer states of Oz or California, but Burgundy, where quality crisp, dry whites can still take on the world and win. Highly recommended, also, are many of the South African Chardonnays, which always resisted using 'oaking' and 'yellowing' as a simplistic marketing ploy.

(Even for the 'oakies', all is not lost. Here's a tip. If you are one of those people who abhor the stickiness of dessert wines, then here, in this much maligned wine area, an oak-aged Chardonnay may well come into its own. Try a glass of Rosemount with your Christmas pudding this year. Wine snobs may mock, but the last laugh will be yours. The fact is, a powerful oaky Chardonnay will cut straight through the most jaded of Christmas pallets. Honestly.)

Chenin Blanc

On a world-wide basis, Chenin Blanc is its own worst enemy. An extremely hardy grape, it tends to be feverishly grasped by grateful wine growers who produce it in mass, low quality quantities, and shunt out oceans of table wine. Not that there is anything particularly wrong with that.

But the French know that Chenin Blanc – boring name, I know – and its natural high acidity, can be used to produce classic whites. How many times have you tasted, say, Vouvray, and experienced that sharp delicious sting at the back of the throat. That's Chenin Blanc doing its thing. However, given that over-harvesting, you really have to go to the Loire to find wines which do justice to the grape. Once there – well, you don't actually have to go there, just purchase wine from that area – Chenin Blanc features heavily in white across the board, from bone-dry mouth-creasing beauties to lush, thick sweet dessert wines to some of the best non-Champagne sparkling wines in France.

Gewürztraminer

Gewürztraminer – let's call it Gewürz shall we? – became famous as the grape of Alsace, that curious block of France that segues into the Germanic. It's a hugely popular area for wine tours. One reason for this, I sense, was that awful prejudice that many people had against German wines. Alsace, it seems, was French enough to hold a certain trendiness.

Well that's all rubbish, really. Whatever its cultural roots, this is a fascinating, beguiling grape blessed with an ability to enchant. You think I'm exaggerating. Please, pluck an Alsace Gewürz-based wine from the shelves, take it home, open it, pour it, and sniff. See, I told you that wine could enchant and surprise as well as intoxicate. Here we find a feminine fragrance, pears and peaches, apples and just a hint of, well, Parma Violets. But the taste that follows is surprising too. Not as sweet as you would expect.

Gewürztraminer can be found in Germany – where it is slightly sweeter – and, more and more, in Hungary, where it is the dominant component in refreshing whites, crisp as a fresh green apple. New Zealand has also taken to Gewurtz, which is a huge and welcome step away from deep yellow Chards.

Pinot Blanc

Another grape that flourishes well in enigmatic Alsace. Extremely popular with those who enjoy cheap but flavourful wine, and there's nothing wrong with that. Alsace-lovers are well acquainted and perhaps make claims for the grape that it can't quite live up to. But for a good table wine with lovely fruity undertaste – especially good for summer picnicking – look no further.

In Italy they prefer to use it as a base for sparkling wines while, more and more, the Californians are now rushing to fill the market with this increasingly trendy grape. (In some of the stark, modernistic wine bars of Los Angeles, where people talk of grapes in the way they once talked about movies, Pinot Blanc is gaining momentum).

Riesling

If we are to assume that Chardonnay is a grape with an image problem, then we must truly pity the poor Riesling. Soon, I hope, a marketing team of genius will grasp hold of this glorious grape and shake all the misunderstandings from the pathetic Riesling myth.

So let's knock the biggest myth of all on the head, right here, right now. When you think of Riesling, do not think of Liebfraumilch. This has been said many times before but it just doesn't seem to be sinking in. Those bottles of Liebfraumilch that we gulped so ferociously in the 1980s, contained hardly any Riesling at all. (And neither did Laski Riesling, strangely enough). These wines were merely aspiring towards Riesling status and, because they were made from a cheaper, less-refined source, they never made it. Riesling, by contrast, has given us some of the finest and most trustworthy wines in the world. The wine snobs, for all their faults, understand this very well. Riesling is often their very favourite grape and, if pushed, they will go on to list the great white wines of Germany and Alsace.

Alsace is the true heartland of the Riesling grape. Here, where the soil and climate really do change dramatically within a few miles, a wide variety of quality Rieslings are produced. However, there has been a steep rise, of late, in the quality of New World Rieslings, which few people predicted. There are some glorious fruity Rieslings produced in South Australia – and these provide a blessed relief from those oaky Chardonnays – which have a refreshing citrus zing. Quite perfect for a summer evening and quite the antithesis of anything that ever came in a Blue Nun bottle. Riesling is also responsible for a few classic sweet whites.

Sauvignon Blanc

For my money, and there's precious little of that, Sauvignon Blanc is the finest white grape of them all. However, I wouldn't listen to me if I were you. The chances are that you will be put off before the glass reaches your mouth. Why? Well, this is probably the oldest joke in the history of wine-tasting. Or, rather, wine-sniffing. Sauvignon Blanc is the 'cat's pee' grape. Like millions of people before you, you may take a sniff and look furtively around the room, wondering where the tom-cat has sprayed.

Wine buffs would laugh at the naive face you pull. But, for once, they are right. You only have to grow accustomed to Sancerre – one of the great wine bar whites – and a number of similar flinty whites to understand the complex qualities of Sauvignon Blanc. Lemon and grapefruit, gooseberry and apple lurk in the backwaters of that taste. A good Sauvignon Blanc wine is about as elegant as wine gets.

The grape has other uses. It lurks mysteriously in the background of no small number of sweet whites. Perhaps most famously it is used in Sauternes, which is still – after all these years – the classic sweet dinner wine.

Semillon

As a grape, Semillon has a patchy history. Only in Bordeaux have the wine-makers stood firmly by the grape, blending it superbly with Sauvignon Blanc. To be honest, that is probably its greatest role, to soften Sauvignon with peach-like lushness. The grape has recently proved popular in Australia and, now that the Chardonnay bubble has burst, could well feature in the next wave of Australian hype. No bad thing, as Semillon has much to offer. Expect

The Main Grapes

a wave of trendily labelled bottles from Hunter Valley.

The main wine grape varieties are ably supported by a whole mass of lesser-used grapes, many of which are mentioned in the following chapter (Second Division Grapes) and throughout this book. These grapes are not inferior ... well, not usually. But they tend to have qualities that either only thrive in specific areas, or are particularly suited to blending with other grapes.

In the world of wine, there is nothing so sacred, so precious, so carefully guarded as the methods of blending grapes. Wine producers will go to great and often ludicrous lengths to protect their secrets. Yes, we know which grapes are included in the blend...mainly because it tells us this on the label. It is fairly obvious what grapes are used in a Cabernet Shiraz. However, often it would take a James Bond of the wine world to find out the methods and quantities used in the blend. Some of this is plain nonsense, but wine producers are a superstitious lot. Many offer tours around their vineyards, but will still not offer the secrets of their particular grapes.

Second Division Grapes

Reds

Pinotage

Lovers of South African wines will be familiar with Pinotage. This is a grape produced by cross-breeding the Cinsault grape – a particularly poor grape variety from the South of France – with Pinot Noir, another rather sneered at variety. The South Africans are clever, though, and now produce Pinotage on a mass scale. The quality is usually good. Pinotage is a name to be reckoned with in the modern wine market.

Petit Sirah

Often found in Californian and Mexican wines.

Periquita

Used a great deal in Portugal, particularly the wines from the south.

Second Division Grapes

Carignan

Used in 'table wine' from the South of France.

Dolcetto

Italy is capable of producing immensely quaffable but undemanding 'table wine'. This, more often than not, is the grape used.

Whites

Viognier

This grape is becoming more and more fashionable although, in truth, it is a rather 'lesser' chardonnay. Some good examples, however, are now coming from Chile and Argentina.

Pinot Gris

Best known as an Alsace grape. Produces smoky, spicy flavours. In Italy it is known as Pinot Grigio.

Colombard

Again, this is known mainly as a grape for 'table wine'. However, if you are a little short of money, it is well worth looking out for. More and more cheap Colombards are becoming available.

Muscat

Often used in sparkly, frothy, Spumanti-style wines from Italy. Nothing fancy. It has a better name in Alsace where it produces nice dry, fresh whites.

Trebbiana

This is a good example of a largely dull grape, widely grown in Italy and Southern France. There may be tiny areas where it makes excellent local wines but they would be very hard to find.

Pinot Noir

A fickle, awkward litle grape which suffers because of its thin skin. When all the elements are working in its favour, it can produce a lovely raspberry aroma and soft, seductive flavours. But it will always be hard to handle.

THE **M**AIN **P**RODUCERS

Once you've learnt to recognize the grape varieties, it's time to move on to the next step and discover the varieties of wine that come from wine-growing regions around the world.

France

There is little doubt that the New World wine-makers have forced the pace in recent years. There is little doubt also that the French, for so long, so entrenched in their traditional methods, fell from their position of dominance during the 1990s. This is particularly true of the ever-expanding quality/mainstream market.

In part, some of this re-balance boils down to shear gimmickry. Designer bottles with designer labels, wine with attractive designer colours even, screamed louder from the supermarket shelves, while the French seemed genuinely reluctant to progress beyond the dusty château-bottled chic that had served them so well, for so long. Even their reluctance to switch to plastic corks, which at first seemed noble, cost them dearly as the percentage of corked wines and returned bottles dawned on wine drinkers and retailers alike.

It does seem, however, that the French have awakened to the marketing realities of the world market. Plastic corks and pretty labels are now flooding in, even from the staunch traditionalists of Bordeaux.

But despite all this, it would still be impossible to begin a run down of wine-producing countries without beginning with France. You just have to. For all the Antipodean glamour, for all the South American exotica, for all the Californian style, you *still* have to begin with France. Whatever the changing markets, one senses that this will always be the case.

French Wine Regions

Alsace

The Alsatians are biting and clawing their way into the market. And about time too. For too many years, the great wines of Alsace failed to get mass-market recognition and remained firmly in the domain of the connoisseurs who seemed quite happy to preserve their secret.

The problem was one of geography. Even people who realized that Alsace was in France, rather than in neighbouring Germany, still seemed to associate Alsace more closely with Germany, or at least, with German wines (which is another issue entirely).

Anyone who has been to the Alsace region will tell you that, in culture, in landscape in 'feel', it is neither predominantly French nor German. It is Alsatian and with that comes a whole batch of idiosyncrasies which the Alsatians proudly and rightly claim for themselves. It's good to report, therefore, that this distinctive culture is reflected almost perfectly in its wine. This is not French wine. (Well, it is French wine *technically,* but you know what I mean.) It's not German wine either.

OK, so you are glancing through the Alsace wines at your supermarket and you happen to notice that they do all seem to have a Germanic look to them. The bottles, the names. Ignore that. Pick something from mid-range upwards (the bottom of the market is, I agree, woeful), and the strong chances are that you will have stumbled across a wine which provides an extraordinarily elegant blending of grape varieties.

The only problem – and it is, indeed, a large problem – is that Alsace producers seem reluctant to let you know if the wine is sweet or dry from the label. Fortunately, a number of supermarkets have become wise to this.

Safeway, in particular, can be commended for the quality of the explanatory tags that adorn their fixtures.

Sample a few Alsatian wines and you will encounter exotic, head-spinning perfumes and sweet, pinky tastes that you would never have thought had any right to be found in wines. Remember Bazooka Joe chewing gum? Well, there's that taste again, lying beneath the peach and berries. The wines of Alsace retain the ability to surprise.

Alsatian wines are becoming increasingly popular, which is one reason why the region is awash with coachloads of wine lovers on tasting excursions. Who can blame them?

The Wines of Alsace

Riesling

Definitely not to be mistaken for German Riesling. It's different, very different. There is a sharpness to German Riesling that is missing here. Older Alsatian Rieslings tend to sweeten and attain a richness that is not normally associated with the wine. This is Alsatian Riesling at its best, autumnal and inviting.

Pinot Blanc

Alsace produces some of the very best Pinot Blanc. Think of apple pie and thick fresh cream. Think lovable lemon lush. The zang of citrus and shock of sweet. Good, summery picnic wine, although a wine buff would probably scoff at that phrase.

Gewürztraminer

Probably the most famous of all the Alsatian wines. The legend lies in the smell. It is strong, some might say pungent! Others swear by the smell. They say it indicates character. Personally, I'd swing towards the latter. The secret does actually lie in that smell. Some Alsatian Gewürztraminer wines have a tang of – I kid you not – those little blocks of toilet freshner. Needless to say, these are not the finer wines.

But if the smell is more exotic – perfumey – then the taste beyond will not disappoint. You will have stumbled across one of Alsace's complex and glorious wines. It is, perhaps, not a type of wine with which to experiment too wildly. Once you have found your favourite, stick with it. It will not let you down.

Muscat

A difficult wine to find. You can go on entire wine tours of Alsace and not hear a mention of Muscat. On the other hand, you may still find an Alsace Muscat lurking in the most unlikely looking wine shop. If you do, please try it. The chances are that you will taste crisp green apples and crunchy green fruit of all types. It will be crisp and dry and certain to freshen your palate. It is excellent as an aperitif.

These wines are all whites. Contrary to popular belief, there is such a thing as Alsace red wine, as Pinot Noir is grown and a drinkable, if fairly shallow, raspberry-like red is produced. It does, however, tend to be on the expensive side and doesn't, frankly, match up to Pinot Noir-based wine from other parts of France and, indeed, the world.

Selected Alsatian Producers

Hugel – Famous and much sought-after wine-makers, responsible for glorious autumnal wines. Rich, golden and the perfect introduction to the kind of characterful wines typical of the region.

Kuentz-Bas – Particularly good if you want to track down the best exotic Gewurtz-based wines.

Albert Mann – The one exception to the rule that Alsace reds are second class. Try Albert Mann's Pinot Noir. Excellent.

Trimbach – Trimbach's Riesling is a delight. Elegant, distinctive and complex.

Zind-Humbrecht – A fast rising star of Alsace. Extremely stylish. The Riesling Clos Hauserer is a must.

Bordeaux

'I live in Bordeaux. It may not have the best wines any more, but it still feels like the heart of the wine world.'

These were the words of famous wine-maker and stationer, Hugh Ryman, when he was confronted by a motley collection of wine-guzzling hacks who had gathered at his château near Bergerac in 1996. It was a strange sentence and seemed to be delivered with a tinge of disappointment. Since then, in many respects, the battle between the traditionalists of Bordeaux and the bold new wine-makers of practically the whole of the rest of the world has been won ... and not by Bordeaux.

The problem still sits on your supermarket shelves. It is this simple. There are still some people who think that a bottle of wine boasting an ancient label with a faded pencil drawing of a romantic French château is automatically going to be a better, purer wine than something in a funny-shaped blue bottle with a pink and green spotted label. Alas, this is not necessarily the case, especially in the low- to mid-price range. Although the name Claret may still carry some weight, the chances are that, unless it is expensive, the Claret in the nice old French bottle will pale in comparison to, say, a similarly priced red from Australia, New Zealand, Chile or California.

Most people have cottoned on to this now and perhaps it's just as well. France, and in particular Bordeaux, has been forced to start fighting the new war. And if that means that some of the traditional methods go by the wall, well, that's not necessarily a bad thing.

Bordeaux is still, in wine-making terms, vast and

unparalleled. And such is the variation of wines on offer that it is essential to break Bordeaux down into regions. If you have always believed that Bordeaux basically produces Claret, and that's it, then, although that notion is understandable*, it couldn't be further from the truth. Here goes.

(It's understandable because it is not your fault. The word Claret has been used as a marketing tool, mainly for sub-standard wines that can't gain any higher appellation. Slap Claret on the label and people will think it is classy. Well, people are beginning to wise up to that.)

Regions of Bordeaux

The Médoc

A thin strip of land which nestles next to the river Gironde. The actual Médoc region is dominated by Cabernet Sauvignon and produces some of the greatest red wines in the world.

Unfortunately, as far as you and I are concerned, it remains unlikely that we will ever be able to afford to even taste them. Small quantities of exceptionally high quality wines are produced by a string of small and incredibly trendy vineyards.

France

Just to confuse the issue. Not only is Médoc the name given to this region, it is also used to cover the appellation which stretches across to the Atlantic Ocean and includes a large region where Merlot takes over from Cabernet Sauvignon. As far as the supermarkets are concerned, this is regarded as the heartland of wines that bear the name Médoc so we might as well go along with it. Especially as these are wines that, being less complex and being produced in much larger quantities, tend to fall within the household budget.

So, they are Médoc but they are not Médoc. Who said this wine game was confusing? The general rule is that, for a reasonably priced Médoc, look for labels that also feature the word Merlot. These will be generally better value and, unusual for French reds, I personally have never encountered a single one that is corked during a ten-year period. Maybe I am just lucky.

If you want to push the boat out a bit, and desire to sample a wine that has greater depth, but don't earn the wages of top sportsman, then hunt for wines which state Haut-Médoc. This is the higher quality Médoc. It's literally higher, too, as the Haut-Médoc vineyards are situated further up the hills, away from the river, where the ground is bone dry and gravelly. Up there, you are back in

Cabernet Sauvignon land and exceptionally trendy villages with enigmatic names like Pauillac and Margaux start cropping up – small villages which feature in every good off licence and supermarket wine department in the western world. Pauillac is generally regarded as the spiritual home of Cabernet Sauvignon. It can be pricey but almost always offers a fabulously complex Claret with a strong tinge of blackcurrant and a slight hint of wood. A particularly good Pauillac – and they are widely available – is enough to make an Australian burst into tears.

Watch out, also, for the village names of Listrac and Moulis on your wine labels. They have yet to earn the reputation of the classic Médoc villages and, as such, tend to produce extremely good wines that will not stretch your wallet. If you can't stretch to Pauillac, pick out one of its less famous neighbours from the same shelf.

Libournais

Based around the town of Libourne, the Libournais region may not have the household recognition of Médoc, but it is universally regarded as the home of Merlot. (Although an awful lot of Cabernet Franc is also grown.)

The central area, and classic Merlot heartland, is

situated just to the north of Libourne at Pomerol. Merlot lovers across the globe seek out the name Pomerol on their labels and there is no reason why you shouldn't follow suit. If you do you will find yourself drinking rich, slick, velvety Merlot with a heady, complex crush of fruits and all kinds of fruity flavours too, cherries and strawberries. The very best, and most expensive, Pomerol is as good it gets, frankly, but down the market the complexity still lingers.

There are plenty of wines from this region that bear the name St Emillion. It is name familiar to many, but not a name that can be trusted. Although many fine wines come from the area, there is little that unifies them in terms of taste and quality. The soil around St Emilion varies from mile to mile and, as such, a huge-ranging variety of wines is produced. The grapes vary like crazy. By rights, Merlot should dominate – this is, after all, Libournais – but often a St Emilion wine will contain a large percentage of Cabernet Sauvignon and Cabernet Franc. All of which makes St Emilion the most bewildering wine region in the whole of France. Recommended wines are listed below, but they may as well come from different planets.

Graves

This is a curious area. Most people think of Graves as a white wine. This is perfectly understandable as Graves whites, which have improved immeasurably since the days of the early 1980s, are now often excellent, and thoroughly justify their place on the supermarket shelves. But the area also produces high quality reds too. Look for the name Pessac-Léognan on the label – white or red – and you will not be disappointed. The reds are particularly flavourful and are now being produced in significant qualities and, as such, seem to be reasonably priced.

Bordeaux Dry Whites

Although the above regions are, with the exception of Graves, mainly noted for reds, Bordeaux does produce a notable selection of whites. It is possible to look beyond Graves for dry whites. Look to any label that features the name Entre-deux-mers (a district, not a château) and a crisp, bright and lovely light white will be yours for an extremely good price. This area has yet to attain the thumbs-up from trendy café bars across the globe. Get in there and get drinking before it does and the inevitable price rise follows.

At the higher end of the market you will find fine whites from Margaux and Mouton-Rothschild. The latter château has been supplying the higher end of the mass market since the mid-1970s and, as such, fell out of fashion for a while. Ignore all that. Mouton-Rothschild whites are particularly excellent.

Bordeaux Sweet Whites

These are far better known than the dry wines. In fact they are regarded as classics. We seem to have been drinking Sauternes for ages – and why not? It is still a gloriously rich sweet wine, bringing a whole variety of tastes to your palate. Most obvious are the honey overtones, but beyond them lie peaches and cream, pineapple and a sharp nutty edge.

The strange thing about Sauternes is that, despite its fame, or possibly because of it, it doesn't seem to retail for the price you might expect from such a carefully produced wine. It's not cheap but, considering its consistent high quality, a bargain. Sauternes doesn't necessarily have to come from the village of Sauternes. It can come from Barsac – just as famous, really – Bommes, Fargues and Preignac. This is nothing to worry about. Although some of the wines might be slightly lighter, quality seems assured throughout.

Selected Bordeaux Producers

L' Angelus – St Emilion. A huge château that made its name around ten years ago and still produces a varied selection of high quality wines.

Clinet – One of the very best affordable Pomerol producers.

Gazin – When French wine went through troubled times in the 1990s, Gazin continued to produce sheer quality. Never prepared to compromise. Expensive but always worthwhile.

Mouton-Rothschild – Often knocked, presumably because it has maintained commercial success since the dark days before the wine revolution. Back in the 1970s it featured on every restaurant wine list. But the wine is consistent and deserves to stand proudly on the shelves.

Trotanoy – A classic Pomerol producer which often sells top-quality wine in the mid- to high-price range. The wines are exceptional value for the special occasion. Look out for this.

Burgundy

During the last ten years, as the rest of France has slipped back into the general market, Burgundy has moved into the First Division. One of the reasons for this is that it seems to have escaped the problems that have become associated with the traditional wine-makers of France and has competed well with New World wines. Some people say this is pure luck, and luck has played its part in producing quality grapes throughout the last decade, but Burgundy's success is probably due to a good many younger producers being open to new wine-making techniques. In short, it is the French region that woke up to the market reality while its neighbours were still slumbering in unsellable traditionalism.

Burgundy Reds

Burgundy is the land of Pinot Noir, the little grape which has powered the world's most celebrated reds. It is, however, a notoriously difficult grape to produce well, which seems to make a nonsense of Burgundy's consistency during the past ten years. In short, Pinot Noir causes endless arguments among producers, all of whom have their own little tricks to tame the grape. But the grape's difficulties do seem to have worked in Burgundy's favour – with a few notable exceptions, New World producers have remained wary of it.

Regions of Burgundy

Côtes de Nuits

The area lies just to the south of Dijon and is a favourite for wine-tours. The best vineyards are gathered on the side of the hill, facing east. This is actually quite a large stretch, from Gevrey-Chambertin along to Nuits St Georges.

Côtes de Beaune

To most people, Côtes de Beaune seems, in terms of geography and climate, identical to Côtes de Nuits. The wines, however, are generally softer and arrive with a gentle alluring perfume. Quite why this should be is a matter of considerable debate, and a pretty boring one at that. Look for Monthelie, which is comparatively cheap and of consistent quality and compares with the vastly overpriced Pommard, which offers the palate a whole jungle of fruit flavours but will empty the purse in an instant.

Côte Chalonnaise

An intriguing area which, while producing a lot of everyday reds, occasionally throws up something that eclipses practically any other red in Burgundy. The problem is, how do you know? Well, look for Givry and Mercurey on the label and you just may have bought a wine that is, in terms of quality and complexity, worth three times as much as you've paid for it. It's a gamble, but those are comparatively reliable villages. If you manage to find something from Michel Juillot's estate, then your luck is in. Buy, enjoy and make it your little secret.

Beaujolais

Let's get one thing straight once and for all. Forget Beaujolais Nouveau. Just forget it, once and for all. We have drunk so much of this vinegary gunk over the years that it has blinded us to just how wonderful good Beaujolais can be. The good news is that the Beaujolais Nouveau thing, little more than a marketing tool to offload wines that, in November, are sub-standard in my opinion, has served to strip Beaujolais of any trendy elements at all. So that's good, because an awful lot of exceptional

Beaujolais is now sitting on the shelves awaiting you. And at a reasonable price, too.

You have probably seen the names, so dip in. Look for the following Beaujolais villages. Fleurie is my personal favourite and, although not cheap, as far away from Beaujolais Nouveau as it's possible for a red wine to be. This is a great wine in which to experience the higher, richer level of red wine for the first time. It is vast in taste and offers a whole batch of contrasting fruits. The same can be said of Morgon. Again it is not cheap and needs to be slightly older. Nevertheless, it never knowingly disappoints. Look also for Brouilly, which hides behind a powerful perfume.

Burgundy Whites

Burgundy whites are the stuff of legend. Burgundy is the birthplace of Chardonnay and it's quite astonishing just how many truly great Chardonnay-based wines have come from Burgundy. The rest of the world, particularly Australia, New Zealand and California, should be on their knees with gratitude, for here's where the story began.

Chablis

The classic bone dry white. Traditionally the absolute perfect accompaniment for fish, particularly shellfish, as it stuns the mouth, helping the flavour of the fish while wiping away any unwelcome aftertaste. There is a lot or argument about Chablis and wine buffs will pontificate for eternity, and perhaps longer, but the fact is that there are no rules. Chablis does vary, and why not? It is almost always good. So why argue? Oaked or unoaked, it retains an elegance that Chardonnays from across the world will never quite match.

You will pay for this, of course, though the price of Chablis has dipped a little in recent years.

Côte d'Or

Look to the villages like Meursault and Chassagne-Montrachet for fabulous whites that are increasingly available. Here you will find a rich, bulbous texture that you always thought was beyond the scope of any white.

For greater value, look for less trendy wines from Santenay or St Aubin. To be honest, Côte d'Or wines are top-heavy with expensive high quality whites that are beyond most people's price range. If you really want to splash out a bit, try Puligny Les Referts or Meursault-Perrières.

Mâconnais

Mâcon Blanc is generally pleasant and relatively cheap, one step beyond table wine. There's nothing wrong with that, but one step above and you reach the Mâcon Villages wines, which have been flooding into the market for some time. Don't resist. The Mâcon Villages whites are almost always delightful, creamy and come with exquisite hints of citrus. Any village will do, seems to be the rule. None are particularly cheap, although the price has softened in recent years, presumably due to competition from the New World.

Selected Burgundy Producers

Armand Rousseau – Many people are now becoming devoted to this producer who maintains high quality wine at comparatively low prices. A great place to start your Burgundy wine adventure.

Comtes Lafon – Now producing whites and reds of genuine affordable class. Look for the Volnay.

La Chablisienne – A huge operation producing enormous quantities of consistently good Chablis. Good value for a class act.

Jean-François Coche-Dury – Hard to find, due to current fashionable demand, but please try. This is the very best white Burgundy and yet remains in the mid-price bracket.

Guy Roulet – Not a lot of people have cottoned on to this producer yet. Excellent, reasonably priced Meursault.

Champagne

Do you love it or loathe it? Regard it as the biggest rip-off in the entire wine world or value its unique ability to instil a sense of the joyous into even the most grim family gatherings? Is Champagne ever really worth the price or are you not wiser to save the pennies and opt for a particularly good Cava, which is something that the television wine experts have been repeatedly suggesting of late?

Well, the truth is that there are all kinds of answers to these questions. Everyone is right and everybody is wrong. Let me explain.

Firstly, everybody has, at some time, been disappointed by Champagne. The problem is that the Champagne that caused you to sneer with derision and mutter words like 'overrated plonk' was almost certainly poor Champagne and you were quite right.

Alas, there is a lot of bad Champagne about. Part of the problem is that some of the Champagne producers shunt the stuff out before it is ready, cashing in on their name. It's self-defeating, and sends the casual drinkers scurrying towards Cava. However, what is absolutely beyond question is that this tiny area of north-east France still produces the world's finest sparkling white wine ... by far. Good Champagne, and by 'good' I do not mean that a bottle has to cost the price of a Mercedes, is still absolutely unbeatable, the most invigorating wine ever made. It has an incredible complexity that is split like a kaleidoscope by its effervescence. You just can't beat it, but you have to be careful.

France

Here are a few Champagne facts. It is an unusual wine that is made from two black grapes – Pinot Noir and Pinot Meunier – and our old favourite, the white grape, Chardonnay. The method of making Champagne is well documented, but still seems strange. A one-dimensional, acidic white wine is produced and banged in a bottle with sugar and yeast. It is then solidly corked and fermentation begins in the bottle. After a few months, the yeast sediment is removed by the most romantic method of all. The bottle is turned upside down, the yeast sediment then drops into the neck and is frozen, the seal is broken, the sediment taken out and a touch of sweet wine added to refill the bottle, which is then re-corked and laid to mature.

Simple? Well, maybe. If you scan the supermarket shelves, you may find a number of other sparkling whites that offer the words, 'Methode Traditionelle'. It will be good, but it won't quite be Champagne. And the reason for that is that, well, nothing else ever is.

All we can do here is offer the pick of the Champagne producers. Please try one. It will change your prejudice and will open your mind to a whole new level of wine. Honestly, it will!

Selected Champagne Producers

Bollinger – Incredibly famous and, as such, something
of a cliché. Never mind. 'Bolly' is lush, loveable,
uplifting.

Charles Heidsieck – Not hugely well known but worth
looking out for before it becomes too fashionable.
Wonderful aromatic 'bubbly' and one of Champagne's
new stars.

Krug – The reputation of Krug is unrivalled. Everything
they produce is executed with absolute perfection.
Expensive across the range but for very special
occasions, perfection!

Lanson – Extremely popular and seemingly ever-
improving in quality, the Black Label is one of
Champagne's best sellers.

Pommery – Seems to specialize in relatively good value,
non-vintage Champagne. Sharp, elegant and fun.

Moët and Chandon – Surely the most famous of all.
Despite selling huge amounts it still manages to
maintain high quality.

Languedoc-Roussillon

The idea that France has stayed too long with traditional methods, and hasn't been prepared to explore not just new wine-making techniques but new and different wines from new and different areas, falls down when we look to the south and, in particular, the Languedoc-Roussillon region.

The revolution in the South of France has increased in momentum during the past decade. Most intriguing of all is the fact that this relatively new region excited the French wine-making world by producing some of the finest wines of the 1990s. A number of wine experts have pointed to the fact that Château Mouton-Rothschild has actively started to move in on the area. Surely a strong indication that the experts now believe the South of France may hold the secret to the future of quality French wine.

Languedoc-Roussillon is, as the name suggests, two regions. Everybody who drinks red wine, I'm sure, has stumbled across names like Fitou, Minervois and Corbières, all of which are based in Languedoc. Nothing particularly new there. But, due to the enterprising cleverness of the producers, it has lifted itself well above the stock table wine market during the past ten years. The Roussillon region is slightly different. Based on the edges of the Pyrenees, the region produces excellent fortified wines in the manner of Portugal. Look for Maury or Banyuls in particular.

Selected Languedec-Roussillon Producers

Cazes Frères – A well-known Muscat producer. A number of wine writers have been pointing towards the Vieux Rivesaltes wine lately, which is largely Grenache.

Font Caude – A name to watch out for. The reds are sensual and velvety and mainly Syrah-based. It also produces Chenin Blanc of note.

Domaine Gauby – A fantastic Roussillon estate that has managed to dig in with the traditional methods and yet make competitive, consistent, hugely complex reds.

Wild Pig – Personally I tend to stay away from these silly modern names and I'm not happy drinking their Fat Bastard Chardonnay or, indeed, Utter Bastard Red, however good they may be.

Château de Lascaux – Look for the very best reds from this producer, in particular a Syrah and Grenache blend that is simply exceptional.

The Loire Valley

The Loire valley has had its fair share of bad press in the past. This is largely due to the fact that, back in the 1970s, it was responsibly for shipping huge quantities of Rosé d'Anjou around the world. A grim, sickly, empty wine it served to hide the fact that the Loire has always produced some of the most diverse and often excellent wines in France. It was just that the French seemed to like to keep them for themselves.

During the 1990s this all changed, particularly with regard to the whites. The was a period when no visit to a wine or café bar seemed complete without a bottle of Sancerre, a wonderful and sophisticated Sauvignon Blanc that helped to put the Loire firmly back on the quality map. And beyond that came Pouilly-Fumé and the Pinot Noir-based wines of Reuilly and Quincy. Hunt for any of these names on labels and, as the quality appears to be wholly consistent, you will enjoy highly elegant wines, blessed with fruity tinges and creamy depths. These wines are leading the French fight-back against the New World Chardonnays and the like. For there is little doubt that they have a sophistication that the big-selling Australians will perhaps never quite match.

Selected Loire Producers

Vacheron – Fabulous crisp and dry Sancerre. Fashionable and can be pricey, but always top class.

Huet – Vouvray producer and good for all things white.

Richou – Once relied on a reputation for white but now produces impressive reds as well. Good, also, for dessert wines.

Domaine de Baumard – Bone dry Chenin Blancs, perfect for fish. Also noted for producing Savennières sweet whites.

Loire valley reds have been less successful, mostly because they have tended to opt for the too much, too young tactic of shunting out table wine. However, in recent years the Loire producers seem to have unearthed the secrets of Cabernet Franc. Indeed, look for this grape on any Loire bottle and, if it is priced reasonably, then it should prove a worthwhile experiment.

Provence

It may be the most glamorous area of France, especially as it includes the Côte d'Azur, but Provence has never been and will never be a classic wine-making region of France. Those wondering if it might jump on to the coat tails of Languedoc-Roussillion will be disappointed.

Some people believe the problem to be nothing more than one of soil and climate. But there is another theory, and a good one too, that suggests that Provençal wine has been spoilt by money. The fact is that the region produces a lot of pleasant wines that will happily accompany an afternoon nibbling cheese in the sun. But the problem is that, for Provençal wine-makers, it is all just too easy to sell. What's more, it sells for more than the wine of any other region of France.

A few wine-makers, noting just how saleable the word Provence might be, especially to people hooked on Peter Mayle books, have started dressing the bottles in all manner of trendy labels. Ignore them.

Selected Provençal Producers

Château Routas – Groundbreaking, tough medicine-like reds.

Domaine Rabiega – Look for the obvious ones from this producer, great Chardonnays and rich moody Syrahs.

The Dordogne

An intriguing area, not least because it is hugely touristic and, of late, the tour operators have started latching on to the fact that the Dordogne is littered with quality châteaux. The good news is that the area is almost an extension of Bordeaux and offers very similar wines, of similar quality that, as yet, can't command the same price region.

I have noticed, in small off licences in England, wonderful oaky Merlots from Château la Jaubertie – which is Hugh Ryman's estate – selling for less than £5 ($7). This is extraordinary value and, as the wine quality is worth double that price, I'd advise you to snap them up on sight. Château la Jaubertie is situated a handful of miles from the lovely Dordogne town of Bergerac, which is now regarded as the pivot of this flourishing wine-making region. But be careful, the Bergerac name does adorn a number of vinegary cheapies that I wouldn't recommend. As a couple of pounds more would secure the aforementioned red, or deep, rich almost black wines from Buzet of Côtes de Duras, then you'd be well advised to splash out.

There are also some absolutely mind-numbingly excellent sweet whites from the region. Look for

France

Saussignac or Moelleux. Best of all though, is the Monbazillac sweet white, again, from the Bergerac region. Here you will find everything you would expect from Sauternes, and more, for a considerably lower price.

On the dry side, the wines of Côtes de Gascogne achieved fantastic commercial success in the 1990s and, from middle market upwards, often proved very good indeed.

At this point, the author pleads for a couple of lines of self-indulgence. It was a Gascogne white wine that, back in 1990, opened his eyes to the wonders of wine and ignited a passion. The wine was Domaine du Tariquet, which has a crisp green-apple base softened by a strong blast of pineapples and a touch of fresh cream. It's still around. Please buy it!

Selected Dordogne Producers

Châteaux la Jaubertie – Hugh Ryman's home estate near Bergerac. Exceptionally good quality simply because the area is not quite in Bordeaux region and cannot command the same prices.

Monbazillac – Wonderful sweet whites from this stunning ancient château.

The Rhône

This is the region that the wine-makers of Bordeaux and Burgundy fear the most. Why? Because it produces wines of consistent quality at lower prices and, most intriguing of all, the Rhône producers don't seem to suffer from bad years.

There are some truly wild reds from the Rhône – intense, leathery, peppery, smoky reds. Strong too, as they

Selected Rhône Producers

Chapoutier – A huge company responsible for the revitalized Châteauneuf-du-Pape, which fell from fashion in the 1980s but, I'm reliably informed, is now one of the top-selling wines in European restaurants. It's good but, knowing restaurant wine prices, not that good.

Colombo – High quality Rhône wines that never seem to show any of the faults associated with the area.

Guigal – Top of the market and, as such, a benchmark that few of us will ever taste. However, Guigal now own Vidal-Flury wines, mainly reds, that are always worth looking out for.

often boast 13.5% alcohol content. Wonderful wines to soften the edges of strong blue cheese and often reasonably priced. Look for the villages of Seguret or Sablet on the labels and hunt, also, for the words Côtes du Rhône Villages rather than the blanket Côtes du Rhône.

Corsica

In the autumn of 1999, the writer of this little book went to Corsica to sample the wine. Peopled laughed. 'Corsican wine,' they said, 'is cheap plonk and only good for sun-stroked tourists.' Since then I have scanned reports from all manner of wine writers and they all seem to agree. Somehow the Beautiful Island just doesn't make good wine.

Oh well. None of those writers were with me, as I sat in the Torriere vineyard, lodged in the mountains, somewhere between Corte and Calvi, sampling reds, rosés and whites. The point is, perhaps, that it is a tiny traditional vineyard, as are all Corsican vineyards and, as such, it is difficult to trace their wines at any but the finest of wine warehouses. Mostly, Corsica does send over shipments of lower quality wine. But look for these producers. The wines are delicate, idiosyncratic and, well, Corsican!

Selected Corsican Producers

Peraldi – From the lovely town of Ajaccio. Rarely seen,
so far, but with a growing reputation.

Terriere – Lodged in the mountains above Calvi. Hardly
known at al, but watch for them on the horizon.

Italy

Good news. The general standard of Italian wine has improved during the past three years. It had to, to be honest. For too long the Italians were sending dull and uninspiring wines across the world; wines with which one could wash down a lasagne, but do very little else. It was a question of character or, more precisely, lack of character. Don't misunderstand me, there have always been fine Italian wines, but your mid-1980s Frascati or Soave, which more or less represented Italy for some time, were never among them.

It's terribly unfair, of course, to put down this fine nation of wine lovers simply because a few dominant and greedy producers cornered the Pizzeria market during the end of the 1970s. Rather like Germany, Italy's commercial success came too soon and too cheaply. Perhaps if, back then, the pepper-mill wielding waiters at the local Italian restaurant had recommended that we drink higher quality Chianti, rather than the standard dull, cheap Valpolicella, then Italy's reputation would have thrived.

Italian Wine Regions

Northern Italy – Piedmont, Lombardy, Venezia, Trentino

Small areas, big wines. It is probably best to begin with Piedmont, an intriguing region responsible for producing rich, dark, plum-like, treacle and high tannin wines, most notably Barolo and Barbaresco. These smell and taste like a classic wine should, and seem to transport you instantly to cities of ancient art and architecture. They are, in fact, profoundly Italian in character and are made, fittingly, from the Nebbiolo grape. They are occasionally rather over-priced, but worth it. Good Friday night wines.

Over on the eastern side of Northern Italy, where the landscape hardens into Slovenia and mountainous Germany, wonderful Pinot Grigios and Sauvignon Blancs are produced, especially from Friuli.

There are good Italian whites, too, especially the Gewürztraminers and Rieslings, which are as good as anything that Germany might offer. Many wine buffs speak of exceptional Soaves from Pieropan, which are increasingly easy to find and seem to be coming down to meet the average wine-buyer's budget.

Italy

From Veneto came Valpolicella and it might be said that we have all drunk too much of that in our time. But beyond the standard lie some exquisite Valpolicellas. The glorious Amarone is a classic example of a wine that has really nudged into the upper end of the market. At entirely the other end of the taste scale is Bardolino, which is perfumey and almost rosé by nature. It is also significantly less intoxicating than the dreamy Amarone, but the choice is yours. The main point is that the word Valpolicella actually covers a wide variety of reds. Personally I believe everyone should try an Amarone, if only once. It's like visiting one of those terracotta-tiled towns that sit precariously on Italian hillsides.

Tuscany

In terms of tourist appeal, Tuscany is Italy's Provence. In short, it is trendy, expensive and British politicians and writers like to go on their holidays there. There is one big difference and, for once, Italy wins over France. Tuscany is generally regarded as Italy's wine heartland. Lying to the south of Florence, it is an area blessed with extraordinary beauty.

If you think of Tuscan wine then you think of Chianti.

As classic as red wine can get. However, contrary to popular belief, Chianti, like Valpolicella, is a diverse and, frankly, bewildering wine. From deep, dark moody reds to light and frisky wines that verge on rosé, all can legally fly under the Chianti banner. The only unifying factor is the tangs of red cherries and strawberries. (The cherries stronger in the richer wines, strawberries dominant in the lighter varieties.)

There are whites from Tuscany but somehow they just don't seem right. Tuscany, if not Italy in general, just seems to reflect itself more in the reds. There is a batch of these reds known in wine buff circles at 'the Super Tuscans'. They are said to head Tuscany's new wave of world-beaters. Well, maybe. Watch out for Tignanello and Sassicaia. These are wines in which the Italians have cleverly blended the local Sangiovese grape with Cabernet Sauvignon. A courageous blending, to say the least, but it seems to be producing hugely complex reds which just may force a new standard in Italian wine.

Umbria, Lazio, Abruzzo

Just to contradict the notion that Italian wines are essentially red, these areas are all producing whites of reasonable quality these days.

Italy

Orvieto is the staple wine of Umbria. Although never a world-beater, it does sometimes have a lightness that makes it the perfect accompaniment for a light fish dish. More famously, Frascati hails from Lazio. Yet again it has to be acknowledged that Frascati is improving. Having said that, it is still correctly regarded as rather bland in character, not at all Italian, if you think about it. The rule, I'm afraid, is simple: there are no bargains here. You get the Frascati you pay for.

Sicily

There are some stupendous cheap wines from Sicily, and most have only arrived on the shelves during the past twelve months. The island's reputation for producing table wines, and little else, has now been superseded. Look out for Inycon Chardonnay that provides sumptuous melon flavours topped by nutty overtones and, right at the end, a lovely hint of vanilla. A great wine to accompany a sunset (I don't know why). Inycon also produce a rich, fruity Syrah, which is surprisingly complex, with leather and tannins rising to the surface. Highly recommended, recently, by a number of leading wine writers and the bottle I tasted last night certainly indicates why. Great value.

Selected Italian Producers

Castellare – Chianti Classico, worthy of the name, especially I Sodi di San Niccolo.

Frescobaldi – Italian perfection, at a price. Centuries of history are piled into these wines, including arguably the finest Chianti Reservas you are ever likely to encounter.

La Parrina – Bold, lush heavy fruit reds that won't break the bank.

Candido – Particularly good for inexpensive silky reds.

Corvo – Sicilian table wine, great value and mostly very drinkable. Great for sitting round the table in vests, slopping pasta and pretending to be Mafiosi.

Taurino – Smooth fruity reds.

Spain

Spain has much to smile about. In many respects it is emerging as the most exciting wine-producing country in Europe. Its resources are vast, paralleled only by France and, unlike France, it isn't constantly bogged down by its own tradition. The Spanish wine-makers have responded well to the challenge from the New World and have been quick to adapt to new methods, both in wine-making and in marketing.

It is true that, during the past twenty years, Spain has flooded the market with cheap plonk. But, like most of the cheap wines mentioned in this book, there have been noticeable improvements of late. This is probably because, even at the bottom end of the market, people are starting to demand wines that are, at least, drinkable.

But Spain produces wines across the board and, at the moment, can compete with any country. What's more, given those vast resources, the future looks bright indeed.

Spanish Wine Regions

Rioja

Any account of Spanish wines has to respectfully begin with Rioja, the most famous of all Spanish wines. Rioja is a region that stretches from the Ebro river, over to Navarra and up to the borders of the Basque region.

There are a lot of young Riojas on the shelves. They are fine but, frankly, a bit of a waste. There are a lot of good cheap red wines in Spain and Rioja is a wine that works better a little up the quality scale. Here it is a vastly more complex wine, simply throwing out a multitude of fruit flavours, and the epitome of fine, powerful, deep-rooted reds. Once you have sampled a good Rioja, you will certainly never go back. Look for Martinez or Cosme Palacio. Torre de Ona is widely available and offers sweet woody notes with damson and vanilla overtones. Look around, though, as the price does seem to vary tremendously.

Navarra

A much improved region that borders on Rioja. In recent

years it has scored a few hits by producing quality reds, similar in taste and complexity to Rioja while managing to keep the price down. As such it is worth looking to Navarra as a suitable alternative.

There are also some fine white wines from Navarra. Look out for the Chardonnay. This is a strange one because it is a comparatively recent addition to the Navarra output and yet, frankly, is a far better wine than the general Navarra whites, which are notoriously inconsistent.

Catalonia

An area in the north-east of Spain, encompassing Barcelona, Catalonia now has a reputation for carrying Spain into battle in the world-wide wine market.

The Catalans are smart and understand all about wine innovation. To appreciate this you only need to look to the proliferation of wines from the family firm of Torres, led by the charismatic Miguel Torres. Their Torres Gran Sangre, a heart-warmingly rich red, is a classic example of a quality wine that has found a mass market, as general sophistication has risen. Torres are based, as are most of the better Catalan producers, in the Penedès region just to the east of Barcelona.

That recently celebrated red, however, is still regarded as something of a sideline in the region which is, after all, the heartland of Cava, Spain's neatly priced alternative to Champagne. Particularly renowned is the the small and rather sweet town of San Sadurni de Noya.

Even after recent price rises, Cava still seems exceptionally good value and it is possible to find a perfectly fine, light and crisp sparkling wine, wonderful for sunny afternoons or, indeed, Christmas mornings at less than a quarter of the price you would pay for a cheap champagne. Priced slightly higher are the Chardonnay-based Cavas, which, apart from being extremely trendy in certain areas, offer a pleasant, creamy taste that, at first, seems unusual for a sparkling wine.

Ribera del Duero

A mix of reds, mainly dominated by the Tinto Fino grape (the same as Tempranillo), flourish from this ancient wine-producing region. Some of it reaches a very high standard indeed, though the prices can be high.

Positive rivalry in the region pits the Tinto Fino purists against those who dare to blend the grape with Cabernet. It is positive simply because the standard of both types of wine seem to be rising constantly. These reds are deeper, thicker, darker and more intense than most Rioja and make a interesting change. It has been said that, due to archaic storage, the proportion of ruined bottles is higher than normal, though personally I have never noticed this.

Central and Southern Spain

The central plains of Spain – Castilla–La Mancha in particular – can be blamed for the oceans of cheap wine which flooded the world for thirty years and continue to do so. In fact, this region filled so many of those basket carafes. In recent years the region has certainly improved its wine-making techniques, but it still concentrates on relatively cheap, though mostly thoroughly drinkable, table wine.

La Mancha is the area to look for if you are just seeking a tasty red to go with a pizza on a Tuesday evening. This is actually something the producers should be proud of. It must be tempting, as the quality rises, to slap a trendy label on it and charge extortionate prices.

There are better quality reds from La Mancha, particularly from Valdepeñas who produce notable lush and cotton-wool-soft reds with strawberry and cream flavours. Valdepeñas wine is reasonably cheap, too.

Sherry

Sherry, even more than Port, suffers from lingering and unfair image problems. In Britain and in the USA Sherry is all too easily associated with middle-class housewives, gathering together in the mornings to gently sip their way into intoxication while spreading the local gossip. Certainly, at the top end of the Sherry market hovers an aura of respectability. And yet Sherry, like Port, is strong, more-ish and heady.

At its best, Sherry is a refined, elegant and delicate fortified wine that really should be making more in-roads into the younger market. (A fortified wine is one that has been strengthened by the addition of a spirit, which is added half-way through the fermentation process.) Unfortunately, it is still largely regarded as an 'oldies" drink.

But the word Sherry covers a large amount of ground. Here are a few of the styles.

Amontillado

Delicate, old and dry. It has a yellowy look and a rich, nutty flavour. Avoid cheap varieties, which will be too sweet and too young.

Spain

Dry Oloroso

Search this out. It is like drinking a fruitcake, with mature berries, cherries and nuts all clamouring to be tasted.

Palo Cortado

This is, at best, balanced somewhere between the above examples. Its pale appearance is backed by a taste that sees the nuts and spices softened by a caramel overtone.

Fino

Fino sherry generally hails from the three great sherry towns of El Puerto de Santa Maria, Jerez and Sanlucar. The sherry from each town is distinctive. Jerez Sherries have a citrus tang while El Puerto makes a harsh, sharper Sherry, which occasionally stuns the unaccustomed drinker. The wines from Sanlucar are often called Manzanilla and tend to be strong and shot through with a yeast-like flavouring.

Selected Spanish Producers

AGE – A massive operation. We have all drunk it at some time although few people realize this. Think of the hessian-covered bottle of Siglo Saco, which found a second life as wax-covered candleholders in downbeat tapas bars. Wine buffs will scoff but, given the right circumstances – the girl, the checked tablecloth, the beach-side bar – Siglo Saco tastes just fine.

Marqués de Cáceres – There are a lot of these about at the moment. Nothing fancy, just good contemporary wines at a reasonable price.

El Coto – Excellent but hard to find Rioja.

Faustino Martinez – Good, solid Rioja and intriguing and improving whites, too.

La Rioja Alta – Another very commercial company that moves huge quantities of Rioja and manages to maintain high standards.

Con Class – Some genuine bargains here. Spicy, zingy white wines including an exceptional Sauvignon Blanc.

Torres – A fast-paced, exciting and innovative company, you will see its distinctive labels everywhere. Glorious red Coronas. Contemporary and reasonable (two words that rarely meet).

Vincente Gandia – From Valencia and apparently favoured by the many football fans of the region and one can see why. The Castillo de Liria range is a perfect example of reasonable priced, lowbrow but distinctive wines. Quintessential Spanish wine.

Selected Sherry Producers

Gonzalez Byass – Actually rather good despite the commercial name. Across the range, Gonzalez Byass continues to prove that commercialism isn't a direct route to undistinguished wines. If you know absolutely nothing about Sherry but fancy a nip, try this. It's in every off licence and yet offers the genuine Sherry experience.

Harveys – The oft-quaffed Bristol Cream is fine for suburban Sherry mornings, but little else. Look for the 1796 range. It is far higher in quality though less famous.

Osborne – Their Fino Quinta is worth splashing out on.

Portugal

Germany's problems with image pale into insignificance next to Portugal, for so long regarded as a country that produces oceans of barely drinkable sub-table wine while concentrating on the best fortified wines in the world.

This reputation isn't undeserved. However, in the 1990s people started to discover that Portuguese wines didn't have to come complete with throat-catching roughness. In fact, at the lower end of the market, Portuguese wines competed very well indeed, offering rich, fruity flavours.

It might also be noted that tremendous improvements have been made within the methods of wine-making in Portugal. Where once it seemed that every other wine would have its taste obliterated by vinegar, these problems have been all but eradicated. Take a chance on a Portuguese cheapie. Now I wouldn't have said that five years ago.

Portuguese Reds

There is a small batch of exceedingly fine Portuguese reds,

most of which are made from the same grapes that are used for Port. Perhaps the best known is Douro, a valley in north Portugal, which produces spellbindingly exotic reds with tangs of leather and spices covering a whole range of fruits. It is the wine that you might expect to come from Portugal. Look out also for the words Tràs-os-Montes on the label. These are Douro wines that have the added ingredient of Cabernet Sauvignon, which blends well with the local grapes like Tita Roriz. These are relatively new and are already adding a much-needed extra angle to Portuguese reds.

Portuguese whites are not as rare and, indeed, as appalling as legend still seems to suggest. Douro, again, produces a wonderful peach-like table wines. True, they will not have the Chardonnay barons shaking in their grape-splattered boots, but they are relatively cheap and delicious (two words that don't seem to like mixing too much). There are also a number of greenish whites that offer a strong floral fragrance and are well worth investigating as, without being complex enough to become world-beaters, they are extremely distinctive and about as far away from a golden oak-aged Chardonnay as a white wine can get.

Selected Portuguese Wine Producers

Quinta da Aveleda – their Vino Verde is accessible and lovely. Look for Casal Garcia, reasonably cheap and will make you think of villages full of terracotta roofs and sun shutters.

Quinta do Cotto – Thick, velvet, syrupy Douro red wines.

Fiuza – Chardonnays that could have come from Australia. Good rich Merlot, too.

Caves Primavera – Extremely commercial and starring at a supermarket near you. Reasonably priced and refreshing.

Sogrape – You may know the name. Remember that Mateus Rosé? It was their fault! Responsible also for some good, mass market wines, especially Douro Reserva Tinto.

Port

Many wine guides do not include Port, believing it to be a completely different experience. Well, maybe, but as more and more people seem to be taking to Port, particularly with a cheese board, it really does merit a mention. Certainly, the region that produces all the Quintas (Port producing estates) in Portugal, has tailored its production towards the drink that they believe to be the king of all wines.

Image-wise, Port it is crawling away from the leather chairs and gentlemen's club tag and seems finally to be moving into the modern world. As it is, in truth, not a million miles away from some of the strong dark reds on offer, it's not surprising that people are taking the plunge.

Port is fortified wine, which basically means that, at a point mid-way in the fermentation, brandy is added. There are a few basic rules:

Ruby

If Port is labelled 'Ruby', then it will – or should – be inexpensive and young. (It has already matured in the wood.) Ruby ports are perfect if drunk fairly quickly.

Tawny

Tawny Port has aged for a long period in an oak cask. It is nuttier than Ruby in flavour and not so good with cheese. It's better as an aperitif and even slightly chilled.

LBV

LBV (Late Bottled Vintage) is actually a single vintage that has been bottled after spending at least five years in the cask. It isn't always good but, when it is, it is perfect! It is intense in flavour, occasionally slightly dusty and, at the top end of the market, hasn't been filtered and, therefore, has to be decanted.

White Port

Well, try it if you must. It can be drunk as an aperitif and is often best served with ice. It's a strange drink that has little in common with the reds.

One of the main problems with Port, rather like Sherry, lies with its strength. Grabbing a bottle and settling down with a cheese board is a wonderful treat for two people. The problem is that Port is flavourful and this often masks its strength. In short, it's all too easy to finish that bottle and start hunting for something else. Indeed, it has been the ruin of many a poor boy ... and girl.

Portugal

Selected Port Producers

Cockburn – Port buffs scoff at the huge-selling Special
Reserve but I see nothing wrong with it at all. It is rich
and dense with deep fruit flavours. Up the range,
Cockburn may make better wines, especially the
Tawny port, but a cheese board and a bottle of Special
Reserve is good enough for me.

Fonseca – Owned by Taylor's, the Bin 27 is fine and
comparatively inexpensive.

Sandeman – The most commercial Port house of them
all. It's pretty ordinary at the big-selling level but climb
the range a little to find good vintages.

Taylor, Fladgate and Yeatman – Classic, unstoppable,
the ultimate Port experience. If you can ever afford it,
do so!

Germany

Will German wine ever emerge from the long shadow cast by the big, bad foursome – Liebfraumilch, Piesporter Michelsberg or Niersteiner – that dominated the general wine market for so many years and fell violently out of fashion in the early 1980s, dragging the whole of the German wine industry down with them? The point is that they were cheap, accessible wines. They weren't bad wines, as such. In fact it was their success in cornering the low end of the market that eventually proved their downfall, as wine drinkers across the world demanded a higher level of sophistication and were prepared to pay for it. Sales of the big three have continued to dive during the past ten years and nobody seems particularly worried about that.

The German resurgence has been talked about a great deal but is still slow to pick up. One of the main problems has been the brilliant success of the New Word wines. If, say, Australia and New Zealand can churn out perfectly reasonable cheap Chardonnays and also offers a range of higher quality wines for not much more – as, say, Rosemount manage on a huge scale – how can Germany compete? Especially as – no fault of Germany this – those wines tell of far-off sunny and exotic places. Germany, by contrast, has a cold feel. What lies beyond this image problem is curious.

Many wine writers, and for many years now, have been telling the world about the high quality and reliable wines of Germany. However, what works for the motor industry doesn't seem to translate into wine sales.

The dominant German grape is Riesling. Although it has struggled to move away from its Liebfraumilch affiliations, it can produce glorious heavily fruited autumnal wines. Now there is a golden rule here. The dry whites of Germany are often tinged with too much acidity and need to be old – five years at least – before they start to soften. The best bet is to stick to the softer, fruity white. Look for a bottle with a high alcohol content of 13 or 13.5 per cent and you will discover a distinctive and lovely German white.

German Wine Regions

Baden-Württemberg

Baden made its name by skilfully producing refreshing, distinctive wines for the cheaper end of the market. Nothing wrong with that, of course, and it could be argued that, within the confines of this price bracket, Baden wines have been among the finest in the world. But, more and more, good quality whites are seeping out from the region. Look for Spätburgunder, which makes a heady alternative to Chardonnay. This could get trendy. By and large, the local reds seem to be expensive and of comparatively poor value.

Mosel-Saar-Ruwer

If Germany has a best kept secret then this is it. Wine buffs have long adored Mosel Kabinett, one of the world's greatest summer wines, but the mass market still seems tentative. There is no reason to be. Take this out on a picnic or to the beach; drink it when it is hot and sunny. It is, I suggest, one of the fundamental pleasures of wine drinking and how ironic that the best German wine is associated with clear sunny days rather than a snowy Christmas scene.

Rheingau

A strange area this. There is no reason why Rheingau, which is a particularly sun-blessed region, shouldn't be producing perfect dry Rieslings. The trouble is that they often fall short of expectation. There are exceptions, but they do tend to lack that extra depth that would put them firmly on the wine map. Good, but not spectacular seems to be the rule. If you do catch a good one, then those Germanic autumnal ripened fruit flavours should seep deliciously through but there will be a certain amount of luck when you purchase.

Pfalz

If there is a German wine resurgence, then it is probably starting in Pfalz, which has stormed to the top of the German wine regions of late. There seems to be a young, innovative cutting edge to the producers of Pfalz and it is expected that they will begin to push deeper into the market during the next year or so. A gathering of sprightly new producers is largely responsible. Look for the fruity Rieslings of Lingenfelder or the joyous Reichsrat von Buhl's Armand Riesling Kabinett, which is utterly contemporary and really should be out there fighting with Australia. Maybe its day will come.

Selected German Producers

Reinhold Haart – What Piesporter should taste like. Packed with fruit flavours.

Karthauserhof – Producers of quality Rieslings with fresh, metallic elegance.

Breuer – Best known for particularly dry Rieslings that zing in the mouth.

Gunderloch – Easy to miss on the shelves, largely because Gunderloch never uses labelling gimmicks. High quality, old fashioned Rieslings which everyone should taste.

Lingenfelder – Lighter than most Riesling producers, floral nosed and great fun.

JJ Prum – Expensive, high class, bold, powerful and elegant Riesling.

Austria

Austrian wine-makers would like it to be known that they never deserved to be placed under the shadow of German wines. Austria has emerged, during the past two or three years, as a sprightly, distinctive and thoroughly contemporary wine-producing country. There, I've said it. Mind you, the wine writers of the world beat me to it by at a good twelve months. Austrian wine has been particularly trendy during this period. Part of this unlikely swing can be put down to people trying new tastes during the post-oaky Chardonnay period and part of it, well, because Austrian wines can be very good indeed.

The key to Austrian wine lies in its uniqueness, or little idiosyncrasies. In particular, there are a bunch of weird and wonderful grape varieties and it is good to see the new breed of Austrain wine-makers concentrating on keeping these unique traditions alive, rather than simply taking more commercially obvious options. The grapes Grüner Veltliner and Blaufränkisch are among these and offer a selection of rare and wonderful flavours.

Although Austrian wines are now creeping onto supermarket shelves, it is a trickle rather than a flood.

What's more, probably because – like Alsatian wines – the bottles have a distinctly Germanic look, they always seem to be dumped in a little huddle next to Germany. Worse still, many supermarkets still only stock a selection of dreadful cheap varieties. The suggestion that this is the core of Austrian wine is rather like saying that Piat D'Or is typical of French quality.

Austrian Whites

When people think of Austrian wine, they think of white wines that touch both extremes. There is, in fact, a bit of a sweet–dry battle raging in Austria and all the grateful drinker can really do is enjoy the best of both worlds.

It seems only natural to mention Austrian sweet whites first. Many of these come from the Burgenland area that sits in the glorious countryside of Austrian lake land. If ever an area produced wines that perfectly reflect the landscape, then this is it. Think of autumnal trees across the hillside. Think of wood-cutting and picnic benches, of ripe apples on a rich deep yellowing sunny afternoon, with wine that flows like golden syrup. The most luscious Rieslings in the world are made in Austria but they are joined by an intriguing array of distinctive dessert wines.

Austrian dry whites tend to be bone dry and, at times, numbingly acidic. People do get confused by this as, naturally, they tend to think of the sweet woody image of Austrian wines. Perhaps the answer lies in the landscape that can be found just a little higher up the hillsides of Austria, where the air is crisp and clear and the colours vivid. Keep this image in mind and think of drinking a stark, bone-dry Gruner Veltliner. There is not a hint of woodiness here, no oak ageing. This is like sucking on lemon peel after eating a whole unsweetened grapefuit. Catch your breath and simply enjoy it. As refreshing as an Alpine scene. Thoroughly Austrian.

Austrian Reds

There are Austrian reds. They are not plentiful but tend to be bold and juicy, like squashed cherries. Some are made from incredibly obscure local grapes and are certainly worth trying if you are in the vicinity. If, however, you are in a local supermarket, you probably won't get the chance. No matter, just try an Austrian Merlot or Pinot Noir instead. They may not compare in terms of depth and complexity with the French, or even Australian reds, but they will have an instant, accessible flavour that everyone seems to like.

Selected Austrian Producers

Freie Weingartner Wachau – As big as they get. Nearly
1,000 small producers cram together in this co-
operative. Incredibly, the quality seems to stay high.
Whites of all descriptions. Don't worry about the reds.

Helmet Lang – Almost completely a producer of heady
dessert whines. Lovely late fruit, all brown and yellow.

Willi Opitz – An intriguing one. Willi Opitz is highly
eccentric and this reflects through all his refreshingly
innovative wines. The sweet whites are unlike
anything else on earth, which must be a good thing.
Watch for a small range of odd reds too. They're surreal
and certain to baffle your guests.

Fritz Wieninger –Viennese wines of great complexity.
Incredibly deep flavoured Chardonnay.

Australia

Well, what can we add to the massive amount of hype and criticism that has hovered over Australian wine-makers for more than ten years. Flying in and out of fashion, they have taken criticism for producing 'gimmicky' wines with trendy labels, they have been accused of hoiking up their prices. But on one thing remain assured, the quality of Australian wine, especially in the mid-range bracket and above, is the most consistently high of any wine in the world.

Modern techniques, brilliant marketing and genuinely excellent wines have helped the Australian revolution. On a personal note, although I never quite fell for the great over-oaked Chardonnay era, I have to admit that, in twelve years, I do not personally recall taking a single Australian wine back to the off licence or supermarket. If you want the assurance of a quality wine at the middle-and-above price bracket, well, you can't go wrong with Oz!

That stated, Australian wine-makers continue to attract criticism. It continues to be suggested that the force which drives their industry is one of commerce, that the wines are guided and flavoured and labelled by scientists and marketeers rather than by people who have a passion for wine. There may be some truth in that but, well, this is the modern world and even the French producers have started to move in the same direction.

Still, you don't need to think about that, as you gather with friends, on a Saturday evening, opening bottles of Wolf Blass or Rosemount. Together you are simply enjoying glorious quality wines. Don't worry about whether some pompous wine scribbler in your newspaper tells you that it is passé to indulge in such Antipodean pleasures. Drink on. Salute Oz and, rest assured, you are far from alone.

The Four Wine-making Regions that Shook the World

New South Wales

Everybody talks about Hunter Valley. Everyone who has been to Australia seems to have been there. Those who have yet to have the pleasure are well accustomed to the region via the wines on their table. It was in Hunter Valley that Australian Chardonnay was born. Rosemount, which makes beautiful, stylish and yet commercially successful wines, white and red, hailed from the Upper Hunter Valley and, although their wings have spread since the heady punkish days of mid-1970s wine-making, they are still firmly associated with the region.

An awful lot of different wines come from Hunter Valley – which, incidentally, has the added advantage of being situated not too far from Sydney – and its place on the wine shelves seems to be getting bigger and bigger. Most people are well accustomed to the Chardonnays but the heavy oakies are now fading fast. One tip might be to opt for Hunter Valley Semillon (various producers are listed below) in which the citrus foretaste is backed up by a deep sensual vanilla ... if you are lucky.

As for the reds. The words Rosemount Shiraz – which might come from South Australia – might seem all too familiar these days, but they sure take some beating. As does the Rosemount Cabernet Sauvignon, which is a minty, vanilla wine with unusual dryness. Look also for Wyndham Estate's Bin 444 Hunter Valley Cabernet Sauvignon which offers medicinal and cedary oak notes, with hints of blackberry, plum and wild cherry.

South Australia

The largest wine-producing region in Australia. All major Australian wine producers are to be found here, although a few, Rosemount among them, still have bases in New South Wales.

Some of the smaller areas within South Australia are now enjoying an international fame that would have seemed incredible just a few short years ago. Most people recognize the name Clare Valley, which is the spiritual home of Australian Shiraz and Riesling. Shiraz features well in the Barossa Valley too. Up in the hills above Adelaide, where the air is cool, some of the finest Chardonnays are now being produced. Set against these surprisingly small regions is the vast, though perhaps less known, Riverland region.

South Australian highlights are many, and are listed below, but it seems necessary to throw in a few names here. Wolf Blass is based in South Australia and should, at some point, be savoured by everyone who loves wine. Whichever Wolf Blass you select, they will not be cheap but, even if your phone gets cut off, they are worth the expense. I recently plucked a Wolf Blass Green Label Shiraz from the shelf of my local Sainsbury's and I can still taste it seven days later. Of greater depth than Rosemount, it was like sitting in a bath of cherries and blackcurrants. The Wolf Blass Yellow Label Cabernet Sauvignon proves a wild and exotic experience. Past the disturbingly dusty nose lies a whole universe of assorted black fruits.

The mighty Penfolds produce here in South Australia. If you get chance to sample the Bin 389 Cabernet Sauvignon or Shiraz, leap at it. Penfolds are always different but always the same. Reliable, supreme quality wines that took on the world and, to a large extent, won.

Victoria

Victoria is probably the most diverse wine-producing region in Australia. It may not have quite the quality names of South Australia or New South Wales, but it does have its moments. It produces a huge amount of cheaper wine, but this is not necessarily wine to be sneered at. Look for the Murray River region on the labels and you may strike lucky.

In fact Victoria is now the only Australian region that manages to produce drinkable wine at a low price. There are a good many small vineyards producing wines of quality. A lot of excellent Shiraz comes from Victoria, especially from the Goulburn Valley. Look also for the Yarra Valley or

Geelong from where a scattering of exceptional Chardonnays hail. As ever with Australia, quality is assured.

Western Australia

A vast region that stretches inland from Perth. It might not be regarded as classic Australian wine country, and none of the huge wine dynasties have chosen to base themselves here. However, that has meant that there are numerous tiny wineries offering high quality and highly individual wines.

It's worth noting that, in terms of distance, land and even climate, western Australia is practically a different country from, say, New South Wales. Wines do flow from the Swan Valley although – look for Margaret River on the labels for quality. This area has a cult following and many wine buffs who scoff at the commercialism of South Australia devote half their lives to seeking out new wines from this area. I wouldn't recommend you go that far but if you see one of the classic elegant Cabernets, or classy Chardonnays that don't try to grasp your attention with vivid yellow colouring, then then you will not be disappointed. The Pinot Noir from Pemberton is also currently making a name for itself. It's not cheap (none of this wine is) but is worth splashing out for.

Australia

Selected Australian Producers

Tim Adams – From Clare Valley. Famous for glorious reds and apple-pie-and-cream Semillons.

Wolf Blass – Some people seem to be irritated by the fact that Wolf Blass sell quality wines, at expensive prices, with a great deal of success. Ignore them. Look for anything, Green Label, Yellow Label and, when you drink it, you will realize that it is money well spent. I wouldn't recommend the more expensive bottles. They have a sophistication that is way beyond my palate.

BRL Hardy – As big as they get. Everyone knows Hardy's Stamp, which has dipped dramatically in price and who's complaining? Under the BRL Hardy banner also come a huge swathe of other Australian wines, Banrock Station, Nottage Hill and Stoenhaven among them.

Coldstream Hills – Yarra Valley producers, responsible for some of the best mid-priced Chardonnay on the market.

Peter Lehman – Barossa Valley wines from across the board. Shiraz and Semillon are particular stars for the mid-price range.

Selected Australian Producers

Penfolds – As I write, I drink from an incredibly addictive, vanilla-tinged Penfolds Koonunga Hill Chardonnay. A favourite and not bad for wine-makers who forged their reputation by producing big, bold reds. Never cheap but always worthwhile.

Orlando – Mentioned here mainly because this huge organization scored highly with the low priced Jacob's Creek, which wine writers loathe while ordinary wine drinking folk, like you or I, see no reason why the words cheap and good shouldn't occasionally meet up.

Rosemount – Beautiful bottles, attractive diamond labels … we all fell for Rosemount in the 1990s, and wasn't it wonderful? Yes, I know, the oaky Chardonnays may be a little passé right now, but Rosemounts were always up there in the just affordable/quite classy bracket. Rosemount also produce incredible sophisticated top-of-the-range wines. We have a lot to thank them for.

Tarrawarra – Another Yarra Valley producer. Good for Chardonnay and Pinot Noir.

New Zealand

It's very tempting to mention New Zealand wines in the same breath as Australian. How many times have we uttered the words, 'Those wines from Australia and New Zealand...' Even elsewhere in this book, I have fallen into that trap. I'm sure that this is much to the irritation of the wine producers of both countries. The revolution in wine producing may have taken place in both countries simultaneously, but they are linked only by the ferocious and positive rivalry they share, like their rugby teams.

Geographically, New Zealand appears to have the lot physically. The soil is often stony, porous, dry and gritty. Sunshine often pours down on the entire island and there is a handy little cool period when the grapes can grow. It could be Italy or even Bordeaux.

This beautiful country produces many wines, but none is more obviously a reflection of its landscape than its Sauvignon Blanc. This is the wine that made New Zealand famous, mostly because it is just so distinctive. Crisp, green salads with hints of lime and lemon. There is something about the Sauvignon Blanc, and, indeed, a few other New Zealand whites, that brings out the individual flavours.

These are great wines for the newly converted wine lover to develop their taste. Perhaps no other wine on earth seems to highlight all those flavours in this separate manner. New Zealand made its name with these lovely distinctive whites.

The reds, however, have been more troublesome for them. While Australian reds soared away in waves of glory, New Zealand reds struggled in the shadows, seemingly incapable of mirroring such glory. Many people thought that this was simply because of New Zealand's comparative coolness. Maybe, but during the past eighteen months the improvement in New Zealand reds, especially the Pinot Noir, has been staggering.

North Island

The most famous and important area is Hawke's Bay, which produces uplifting sunny Chardonnays, crisp Sauvignon Blancs and deep red Pinot Noirs. Look for the Hawke's Bay Sauvignon Blanc from Delegat's wine estate, which is one of those crisp salad and gooseberry classics (ditto Morton Estate Hawke's Bay Sauvignon Blanc). In the mid-1970s a lot of dull bulk wine came from the Gisborne region, but it has lifted itself from the shadows of late and

New Zealand

now produces the richest, creamiest Chardonnay in New Zealand. For Chardonnays and Pinot Noirs, look also for the name Martinborough, a pretty town with a growing wine reputation.

Selected New Zealand Producers

Cloudy Bay – Part Australian owned, but New Zealanders will forgive even that. The Sauvignon Blanc is a classic (see below). The Chardonnay is almost in the same bracket. Look also for the plummy Pinot Noir.

Dry River – Wow! Expensive Pinot Noir that could fell a French aristocrat.

Grove Mill – Produces a rather nice selection of flowery whites. The Riesling makes an interesting contrast to anything produced in Europe. Good for Gewürztraminer too.

Hunter's – Very famous, mostly for the oaky Chardonnay that is more complex than that simple description suggests. Good, accessible Sauvignon Blanc as well.

Jackson Estate – Noted for the constantly improving Riesling.

South Island

Those who think that New Zealand is a land with a long history of wine production might like to note that, on the South Island, wine production only began in 1976. This is particularly surprising for those who are devoted to Marlborough Chardonnays, Rieslings and Sauvignon Blancs which all deservedly gained intense followings during the 1990s. Within twenty years, they were regarded by many as classics. A quite remarkable achievement.

As well as that happy trio, there is some very fine Pinot Noir, especially around the Christchurch area. When I pressed a New Zealand-based friend of mine to recommend a particularly good locals' wine, he told me about Marlborough Cloudy Bay Sauvignon Blanc and seemed quite upset when I told him that we had been drinking it for years. His reaction is apparently typical as New Zealanders come to terms with the fact that their wine, on a global scale, is significantly more famous than their All Blacks rugby team … and considerably more elegant.

South Africa

The revolution in South African wine producing, and the rest of the world's eagerness to drink its wine, has been nothing short of stunning. On a world-wide scale, this explosion began in the early 1990s and continued to gain momentum into the new century. In terms of expansion, South Africa is the wine success story of the past decade.

However, South African wine has not attained the latter-day trendiness of Australian or Californian wines. There is one basic reason for this. While South Africa has been so effective in supplying to the lower- and mid-priced wine area, it has not produced the higher quality wines in any significant quantity. There is, of course, some very fine South African wine around but you still have to hunt for it.

South African Red Wines

Many people look to Stellenbosch as the benchmark of South African red wine quality. It is certainly the region that has the best reputation. Unfortunately, there are too many producers who hang on to this reputation while producing lesser wines with overpriced tags. However, the best red wines in South Africa still tend to come from this region. Cabernet Sauvignon dominates, but is often joined in the blend by Merlot and Shiraz. Long Mountain is one of the more visible producers of Cabernet Sauvignon and their lovely cassis-heavy wines have attained a cult status of their own. Look also for Mount Disa Cape Salut which offers a burning blackcurrant wine that takes some beating.

Down in the Cape region, the producers have cross-bred Pinot Noir with the grape Cinsault, which resulted in the celebrated Pinotage grape. This process has a long, deep history, stretching back to the 1920s and is an entirely South African tradition. From Pinotage come the very best South African reds. Full of plums and raspberries, spices and leather...an evening with a good South African Pinotage is latterly regarded as a classic wine experience. There are also some good examples of Ruby Cabernet wines, which are velvety and lush. Too shallow, perhaps, to seriously challenge the French equivalent, but now becoming more prevalent on the wine shelves.

South African Whites

Although there are a great many Chenin Blancs in South Africa, they have been joined in recent years by large amounts of the grape Colombard – particularly successful in the low price range – Cape Riesling, Sauvignon Blanc and, of course, Chardonnay. The general quality is still rising and South Africa's reputation for producing whites with no depth whatsoever is now receding.

It was the Chardonnay that certainly helped kick things along. Many people were surprised that, during the great era of trendy oak-aged Chardonnay being slapped on every cool wine bar table in the western world, South Africa were quick to join in the gold rush, 'all of a sudden' producing deep yellowy wines in cool-looking bottles. We didn't really know what they were, but we drank them anyway. Thankfully, now that good sense is prevailing, the better South African whites are rising to the surface. There are actually a few highly sophisticated and invigorating Chardonnays, particularly from the Robertson region.

Look out, also, for the higher bracket Sauvignon Blancs which hail from the cape and are beginning to mirror the crisp, dry, green apples appeal of many of the wines from the Loire.

Some of the other intriguing regions to look for are:

Paarl: Emerging from the shadow of Stellenbosch, Paarl is now heartily churning out good quality Chardonnays.

Although personally I have purchased more than a couple of astonishingly characterless whites from this region in the past, I am assured that techniques are rapidly improving and that I have just been plain unlucky.

Franschhoek: A region of Paarl although it often prefers to ignore that fact on the labels. Look for some exceptional Sauvignon Blancs from this area. Somehow, the local producers have hit upon a winning streak and quality seems assured.

Elgin and Walker Bay: It's difficult to wander around a supermarket wine department without stumbling over whole areas of South African wines dedicated to Elgin and Walker Bay. These are particularly sought after these days. I even saw a café bar hosting an Elgin event in Liverpool! But be careful and ignore the hype. Yes, these coastal regions are doing interesting things with Chardonnay and Sauvignon Blanc, but the wine writers who, in the late 1990s, wrote about this being the cutting edge of wine innovation were, frankly, wrong. The wines, as listed below, are elegant and supple and certainly worth tasting. They are also reasonably cheap, but they are not carrying white wines onto a new level!

South Africa

Selected South African Producers

Dieu Donné – South African Chardonnay came of age
  with this producer. More laid back than its Australian
  competitors, it scored a hit when people began to tire of
  that oakiness. They do a fine Merlot, too.

La Motte – Good for Cabernet Sauvignon and Shiraz. The
  wine buffs have been picking up on the Sauvignon
  Blanc, lately but I have failed to locate a bottle.

Springfield Estate – A winery that is new even by South
  African standards, it has made giant steps of late.
  Excellent, elegant Chardonnays and a selection of
  clever and distinctive reds.

Mulderbosch – Probably produces the best Sauvignon
  Blanc in South Africa. Mulderbosch are also responsible
  for making the kind of Chardonnay that still turns
  heads.

Stellenzicht – Huge range, widely available.
  Stellenzicht's best moments are probably reserved for
  the reds. A friend of mine swears by their Pinotage and
  who am I to argue? The Shiraz is wild and rich.

Warwick Estate – Personally I'd opt for the Warwick
  Estate Pinotage every time. Awesome and within
  budget. Also produces a mighty Cabernet Sauvignon.

U.S.A.

California

As you might imagine, Californian wine-makers have the world of technology at their fingertips. So much so, in fact, that, rather like Australia, they have often been charged with making wines scientifically to suit the markets. Fifteen years ago this may have been the case but that is one problem that actually sorts itself out, given time. The fact is that, as wine lovers across the globe have increased in sophistication, so the world's most astute wine producers have had to raise their quality accordingly. This is the cynical view but, as the end result is better wine for all, nobody seems to be complaining.

There is still a slight problem with Californian marketing. They are so slick, so hip, so astute that there is an occasional tendency to hype a wine so much that it floats into a price bracket higher than it deserves. Most Californian wine is actually quite expensive these days. They get away with it simply because we are prepared to pay more.

Many people believe that Californian Chardonnay is

the finest in the world. Well, maybe. It certainly is distinctive. The Californian wineries, particularly from the Napa Valley, always managed to produce Chardonnays that held a peach flavour strong enough to fend off the oak. As such, they remain in fashion.

Whether the Sauvignon Blanc has ever been so fashionable or not, is a matter of some debate. During the 1990s, it certainly didn't match up to the Chardonnay. Indeed, there can be few people left on earth who haven't enjoyed a Gallo Chardonnay. (In true American style, so massive is the Gallo winery that it alone produces more wine than the whole of Australia. Many people followed Gallo upmarket from those carafe style bottles of dull cheap Chardonnay to the finer Turning Leaf.)

On the red side, Cabernet Sauvignon is the grape, again from the Napa Valley, that established California as a major wine-producing area. (Ironically, given America's accent on size, the Napa Valley is only twenty-five miles long.) The complex nature of the Cabernet Sauvignons has certainly intensified during the past ten years and now it is possible to sample wines of velvety pluminess topped by hints of mint. Particularly good are the Cabernet Sauvignons of Fetzer. Pricey but always exceptional.

Californian Merlot is, to be honest, not quite in the Cabernet Sauvignon league. Apart, that is, from right at the top of the range. If you fancy shelling out serious money then you will be able to taste a Californian Merlot that equals all but the very best that France can offer. Most people just smile and opt for something cheaper and perhaps more exotic, like Californian Zinfandel. Wild and free and very Californian. In the grape section I referred to it as 'the punk grape' and that cap does seem to fit.

Other American States – The Best of the Rest

When one thinks of great Californian names like Fetzer, Acacia, Gallo, Ravenswood, it's easy to dismiss the rest of the USA wineries as also-rans. To be honest, this is largely true. Obviously, California has the perfect wine-producing climate and, frankly, the extreme shifts in climatic conditions in many other areas are hardly conducive to making great Chardonnays or rich Zinfandels. But there are exceptions. The wine-making industry in Oregon – actually started by Californians in the 1960s – has flourished, lately, presenting the world with strongly flavoured Pinot Noirs and some truly individual sparkling whites. (Look for Oregon Gewürztraminer sparkling white for a truly unusual and quirky little number. Bound to confuse that wine snob who always pops round on Fridays, condemning your choice of wine while drinking you out of house and home.)

Look also, and you will have to look hard, for wines from Washington State. In particular, from the Yakima and Columbia River valleys. They're not easy to find, but it's worth hunting for their fine Chardonnays and Merlots.

Selected USA Producers

Fetzer – This massive commercial winery never produces poor wine. It's all superb and well worth the extra bucks.

Gallo – Very famous and, as previously stated, massive. The Turning Leaf wines are a particular favourite around here, trendy bottles and all! Slightly less desirable is the Garnet Point range.

Crichton Hall – The Chardonnay is massive in taste. Some might call it vulgar but, on the right night, with a rich fish dish perhaps, it can seem incredibly refreshing. This British-owned Napa Valley winery also produces a velvety Merlot.

Selected USA Producers

Robert Mondavi – Could possibly lay claim to being the instigators of Californian wine production. Not known to let the grass grow under their feet, Mondavi are still innovative and searching for the next big thing. (A great oaked Sauvignon, by the way.) They may be fired by commercialism but it is good to see a producer driving the industry ever forward (which, of course, is the American way). Responsible for the Woodbridge group of wines which are refreshing, if rather shallow.

Ravenswood – Deep, dark, exotic, jungly Zinfandels.

Sanford – I discovered this winery many years ago, when on holiday in Santa Barbara. It specializes in full-flavoured wines. Chardonnay, of course, but the Pinot Noir is absolutely stunning.

King Estate – A huge producer from Oregon noted, especially, for Pinot Noir.

Staton Hills – From the Yakima Valley, this winery produces a mighty Cabernet Sauvignon and little else.

South America

Mexico

The growing reputation of Mexican wine, which almost all comes from that funny little Baja Peninsula, is largely the responsibility of La Cetto. It's very unusual to see just one country producer making such a fantastic impact. Somehow, without hype or reputation, those simple La Cetto labels started screaming at us from the wine shelves in the early 1990s.

How lucky, for Mexico and for us, that La Cetto produce such glorious spicy and full-flavoured Petit Syrahs, quite perfect for quelling the bite of tacos and chilli! Confusion sometime reigns because La Cetto is distributed from a Californian base and, as a result, many people believe it to be Californian. Not that it makes any difference.

Chile

At the lower end of the market, Chilean wine is a runaway success story. It's at that point where French, Italian and Spanish wines dip into the table wine section and seem to use that as an excuse for all manner of horror bottles. Australia and New Zealand have lifted themselves above that market, no doubt believing in the greater prizes that come with quality production. It's almost as if Chile has taken one step backwards, and has unleashed a small but stunning selection of cheap wines that are still fruit-packed and certainly rarely fall into the dusty trap of their Bulgarian competitors.

Quite how they have managed this is something of a mystery. One might have expected a drop in quality from a country whose production has risen tenfold in ten years, but no. If anything, while the prices have been pegged, the quality has risen.

There is one curious factor regarding Chilean wine. The country offers a diverse landscape and wildly varying climate. None of this, however, is reflected in its wines, which appear to be remaining curiously uniform. Still, that's a mild grouch. After all, this is the country that has produced heady blackcurrant Cabernet Sauvignons topped by a delicious and refreshing hint of mint. From other countries one might reasonably expect to pay rather more for such an experience. Better still is the Chilean Merlot, which is more complex and offers dense herbal flavouring.

Some of the producers have attained great fame. It's difficult to imagine, for instance, the last five years without

South America

Selected Chilean Producers

Concha y Toro – Continues in a line of high quality wines, especially under its own name. Also owns the Trio and Explorer ranges. Good quality throughout.

Cono Sur – The name used to put people off, and then they tasted the wine. Excellent and fairly reasonable, especially the Zinfandel and Pinot Noir. Actually owned by Concha y Toro, and responsible for the Isla Negra label which has been selling consistently for a number of years.

Errazuriz – I always liked this winery, especially the mid-price range. The reds and whites seem equally good. The Syrah is a massive seller, proof that the general wine buyer is now quite comfortable with Chilean wine.

Miguel Torres – Always distinctive and certainly responsible for pushing Chile onto the world stage. Still producing good, reliable, reasonably priced reds.

Underraga – Better for the whites, with a fine buttery Chardonnay the best of the bunch.

Valdivieso – Yet another producer that has been extremely successful with low- to mid-priced reds, especially the Pinot Noir. Surprisingly, they are better known for sparkling wines back in Chile.

Errazuriz Syrah, Cono Sur or Valdivieso Merlots. Three examples of perfect low-priced wine.

Chilean whites are less renowned, although, in quality and price, almost perfectly mirror the reds. Errazuriz Chardonnay is a classic example, full of citrus and jungle tinges, while the Sauvignon Blancs seem slightly too sharp, too frosty to be taken seriously. There is Gewürtraminer as well, which usually comes from the Bio Bio region and can be disarmingly excellent.

Argentina

Here's something that will amaze you. Argentina is the fifth largest wine-producing country in the world. The wine of the Andes, as they say, is flooding the world, and it's no bad thing either. The warning is out: if the top-notch countries – France, Italy, Australia – don't keep their quality levels high, then Argentina, the dark horse of international wine, could well creep up on them.

Argentina, for many years, has been the South American wine industry's best kept secret. It surprises many to discover that, for example, the Etchart vineyards have been producing wines since 1850. This is the perfect example of an Argentinian producer with a long legacy that hasn't been afraid to move into the modern age. Argentinian wine is nothing if not contemporary.

Most of Argentina's wine comes from the Mendoza, an extraordinary and beautiful city sitting in harsh desert land. From Mendoza we have been given luscious Argentinian reds – in particular, Malbec. Malbec, at its best, is dark, velvety, sexy and brimming with black plums and liquorice. By contrast, the Argentinian Cabernet Sauvignon is less easy to define. Quality and taste do vary wildly. I'd stick to exotic Malbec.

Selected Argentinian Producers

La Agricola – Entertaining wines from an innovative large producer. Many labels come from this house, particularly noticeable are Santa Julia and Picajuan Peak. Look for the Bonarda/Sangiovese.

Etchart – These wines been very prevalent on the shelves lately and have been picking up some excellent reviews too. The Malbecs are excellent but look, also, for the Cafayate Torrontes, spicy and rounded. Trendy labels, too.

Navarro Correas – Extremely good and complex reds sold at stunningly low price. The Merlot is particularly fine.

Odds and Ends

As wine-making techniques improve the world over, and as logistics improve too, so oddball wines – normally clumped in the 'Other Countries' of the wine shop or supermarket – are gaining shelf space. Some of them can be very good too and, as the general palate improves, there is surely going to be a constantly increasing demand for more unusual wines from exotic and distant places.

Bulgaria

There is a problem here. Many people, myself included, have stumbled into off licences armed with the last few pounds of the week's budget only to emerge with a Bulgarian wine that looked so promising, so exotic and lacking in gimmicks as it sat on the shelf. Then, once home, the true awfulness of the wine begins to sink in. It's not that there is anything technically wrong with it, it just tastes so dull and lifeless. As it took care of your last fistful of pennies, you drink it anyway in the forlorn hope that some flavour might start to seep through. And, as it happens, it does improve, slightly, by the third glass.

Odds and Ends

Selected Bulgarian Producers

Rousse – Good quality wines from the unlikely north ... so far north it's almost Romania. Hefty, voluptuous reds.

Domaine Boyer – One of the early Bulgarian stars, now looking a bit lost in the modern world.

The problem isn't your taste buds. It isn't the Bulgarian wine-makers, either, who are generally a clever and learned bunch who, still in a post-communist state of reclaiming the land and the vines, are trying to supply a modern sophisticated market with vineyards that are, at best, ramshackle. It is slowly getting better and the potential for Bulgarian wine is immense but it is going to be a long process. It isn't really the cheap bottles of wine that are at fault. They genuinely are improving and are now of reasonable standard and show just a little more depth than table wine. But rise up the scale and decent wines are extremely thin on the ground. Your best bets are the Cabernets from the Oriachovitza region.

Hungary

Hungary is one of those countries that are slowly but surely creeping up on us. This is partly due to wine-makers like Hugh Ryman who, although based in Bergerac, has been extremely active in cultivating Hungarian wine since the fall of the Iron Curtain.

There is nothing dull about Tokaji. Fine dry exotic white, with strong lime overtones, made from the exotic Furmint grape. Wonderful for those seeking something light but different and quite perfect with any kind of oily fish. Look for Hungarian Chardonnays from Balaton which are drier than you would expect, with crisp, peppery overtones. A far more refreshing wine than you might be expecting. Hungary, like Bulgaria, is waking up from a reputation of dullness.

There is also a whole range of sweet wines from Tokaji, and they are increasingly turning heads and grabbing column inches, with their deep autumnal and honeyed flavours. A Hungarian evening, with the dry whites during the meal, and the sweets to relax with during dessert, is thoroughly recommended. Hungary's red wines are getting better, too. Hugh Ryman is no fool.

Odds and Ends

Selected Hungarian Producers

Milne and Co – An outsider or 'flying' wine-maker, now
  producing the rich Chapel Hill Cabernet.
Neszmély – Look for their Sauvignon Blanc.
  Unbelievably elegant.

Romania

Hard to track down at the moment, as few supermarkets
seem willing to give Romanian wine a try. An increasing
number of Romanian wines are becoming available in wine
warehouses however.

There is a problem. It's not that Romania is incapable
of making good or even excellent wines – Pinot Noir,
Cabernet Sauvignon and Merlot are all used in many
mature grapes across Romania, and reports suggest that
local wines can be exceptional – but an initial wave of
Romanian export wines in the mid-1990s saw very little of
this quality and the country gained a reputation for dull,
dusty and poorly produced reds.

Look for Prahova Cabernet Sauvignon or any
Romanian label that carries Merlot. It will be a gamble
but, hopefully, one where the odds will increasingly be in
your favour. One for the future, really.

Slovenia

In 1996, on the banks of beautiful Lake Bohinj, I personally sampled an exceptional Sauvignon Blanc from Slovenia's Slava Valley. It was a revelation for me as, like most people, I had dreadful memories of swigging dreary Laski Riesling from Slovenia in the early 1990s. If you encounter a few bottles of Slovenian wine on the shelves, look for that Slava Valley name. If not the Sauvignon Blanc, there are a number of slightly sweeter whites being produced. A few bigger producers have been researching in Slovenia of late, probably in search of an exotic name from some remote village which can be bottled to resemble the height of fashion.

Greece

Is interesting to note that wine from Greece is now being stocked in numbers comparable to German wines. Incredible really, for a country with such a dubious reputation for wine. Although people are now warming to Greek wines, most people tend to still regard it as 'holiday wine'. The kind of stuff that taste wonderful in your beachside taverna in Crete, but seems to gain in acidity during the flight home and, once back, is rendered completely undrinkable. No one knows why.

Greece is producing some good, custardy whites at the moment. Look for Moscophilero on the label, which can be sweet or dry and has richness that one might not normally associate with Greece. It is Muscat-like and quite enticing. There are a large number of other Greek whites currently gathering on the market, and the quality, though never outstanding, is always excellent for wines in the mid-range category.

The situation is similar for the plentiful reds, which seem to sit nicely in the low- to mid-price range and are comparable to, say, Portuguese reds. A good trick is to ask a wine buff friend to taste Greek wine blind. I can't believe that many would guess the correct nationality. Maybe that's a bad thing, as Greek wines are not strong on individuality.

England

English wine has traditionally had a very poor reputation, but things have certainly changed for the better during recent years. More sophisticated wine-making techniques, plus a new wave of determined wine producers has turned the tide. There are ways and means of dampening the acidity and allowing the natural fruit flavours of English wine to shine through.

England will never seriously challenge any of the top wine-making countries, however. The weather is simply too unreliable. The hardy grapes of English wine – Schinburger, Reichensteiner – are never going to supply much in the way of complexity, but the wines are at least indicative of English summers, with flavours of gooseberry, nettles and apples fighting for dominance, all topped by the vivid smells of English gardens. There are no reds of note, so it's mainly summer picnic style stuff.

Incidentally, ignore anything that proclaims 'British Wine'. British wine, as such, is almost always low budget, bland-to-utterly-tasteless or over-sweet stuff that has been made from imported grape juice and, therefore, owes nothing to the English countryside. There are 380 English (and Welsh) wineries in operation, producing ninety-five per cent white wine. The Welsh wine industry is tiny but has been getting some reasonable press of late.

Odds and Ends

Selected English Producers

Denbies – Large estate noted for the Pinot Blanc and a range of sweet whites.

Breaky Bottom – Courageous wine-makers squeezing a genuinely fine wine from the unfashionable and unsexy Seyval Blanc grape. Excellent and lush.

Sharpham – It's difficult not to like this wildly innovative producer which has scored recently with the extraordinary Beebliegh red.

Turkey

Why not? There is an awful lot of wine produced in Turkey but most of it stays within Turkish shores, which is probably just as well. However Sainsbury's do occasionally stock white wine from the Villa Doluca winery which is generally a good standard for a mid-price. Like Greek wine, it doesn't seem to reflect the local landscape or climate, but is worth looking out for.

Canada

Canadian wine-makers would probably be incensed at being put in an 'odds and ends' category. In ten years' time, such a thing will surely seem absurd. By then, I sense, we will all be firmly acquainted with the sizeable Canadian section on the wine shelves. For the moment though, and for much of the world, including most of the USA, Canadian wine is indeed an oddity.

The Canadian wine industry is extremely young and, as such, a number of mistakes have been made. But comparisons with, say, New Zealand in the late 1980s, which have floated around the wine press lately, are not really relevant. The technical aspects of wine-making have become increasingly sophisticated and problems in mass production can be found and sorted very quickly these days. But it isn't just a scientific problem, it's a marketing problem too. If Canadian wine is going to become fashionable and widespread, then it first must find and exploit a niche somewhere in a crowded market. On a basic level, will a bottle of, say, a Canadian Riesling evoke an image of the beautiful Rocky Mountains or the dramatic expanse of Lake Ontario? Maybe. Selling wine is as much about image as anything else. The future looks interesting.

Most Canadian wine comes from the area around Ontario. It's predominantly a white grape region, as you

Odds and Ends

Selected Canadian Producers

Château des Charmes – From Ontario. Look for the St David's Bench label, particularly the Cabernet Blanc and Riesling.

Henry of Pelham – Not just responsible for the Merlot mentioned above. The Cabernet Franc is heady, aromatic and very rich.

Mission Hill – This producer has been making good progress in commercial terms lately so expect to see its labels, particularly the 49 North reds and white. A good bet for a different Merlot.

might expect, although the reds are on the march. The aforementioned Riesling really could become something of a groundbreaker. Sweeter than their German equivalents, the Canadian Rieslings have, thus far, gained a patchy reputation. But that sweetness isn't as clumsy as a few experts have suggested and, once the taste gets around, they could just catch on. Waiting in the wings are Pinot Blancs and Pinot Noirs of quite acceptable quality. Coming soon to a supermarket near you, as they say. Look for the lovely, buttery Chardonnay from Southbrook Farm.

On the red side, things are at last improving. Canadian Merlots and, especially, Cabernet Sauvignons have been rather scoffed at in the past. But they are getting their act together now. Henry of Pelham Merlot is one particular red to look out for.

RECOMMENDED

WINES

Wine

'Oh no! Not another wine list. Please, please no!'

Don't worry. I know how you feel. There are wine lists everywhere, in supermarkets, in wine warehouses, many of them completely contradicting each other. It's irritating, confusing, unsettling. What's more, most of them are designed solely with the intention of promoting particular sections of the stock of that supermarket, that off licence chain or wine warehouse.

Well, I have no such agenda. This is just a simple list that can be used as a quick-glance guide. It doesn't necessarily correspond with the wine recommended in the rest of the book. The reason for this is straightforward. I didn't want to simply repeat myself. Some of the wines listed are unusual. They just are names to look out for. Others are names that you will encounter every time you glance at a wine shelf. You couldn't, for instance, wander into a wine department and not notice words like Rosemount, Fetzer or Wolf Blass. This is fine by me, as all three are splendid wine producers who have helped lift our tastes into a new dimension.

But their French counterparts, although producing wines just as fine, if not better, do not seem so visible. It

Recommended Wines

could be that there are simply more of them, which is indicated in this book, and they do tend to huddle together in one massive 'French' section which can be a bit daunting. Personally, I just think that the Australians, Californians, New Zealanders etc. are still better schooled in the art of marketing. The cynics may scoff at those flash trendy bottles, but at least they make the task of deliberating over which wine to buy more fun. I defy anybody not to become bored, sleepy even, when confronted by rows and rows of identical, unreadable, dusty wine bottles. This is the modern world. Style, be it in the composition of the wine, or in the design of the bottle and label, is very much part of it, so let's enjoy it.

This list is simply a guide to assist in the perusal of the wine racks. All the wines are priced in the middle range. I don't personally see any reason why anyone should go higher than that bracket. There are some cheap wines that are perfectly acceptable. However, the general rule does suggest that, if you stay in this mid-price bracket, the chances of encountering a 'bad' wine are now very slim indeed. There may be a few dull wines around, but none are listed below. I'm afraid I have to admit that I can personally vouch for that!

New World

Australia

Reds

Lindemans Cawarra: Shiraz/Cabernet. Thick with blackberries, raspberries, topped by spices.

Lindemans Bin 45: Cabernet Sauvignon. Black, hearty with deep berry aromas topped by a sting of nettles.

Lindemans Bin 50: Shiraz. Spicy overtones, rich fruit and oak finish.

Mirrabroo: Shiraz/Cabernet. Penfolds made, and it shows. Extremely elegant blend with blackberries and blackcurrants fighting for prominence.

Noble Road: Shiraz. Sting of blackcurrants with a long fruity finish.

Oxford Landing: Cabernet/Shiraz. Yalumba (a Barossa-based company who produce Oxford Landing and Coonunwarra). Purple-coloured and aromatic. Cherry and blackberry flavours.

Penfolds Koonunga Hill: Shiraz/Cabernet. The blackcurrant wins out in this one, topped by dreamy oak.

New World

Peter Lehmann. Barossa: Shiraz. Rich, dark, moody and full of exploding spices.

Rosemount Estate: Shiraz/Cabernet. Cherries, plums and a curiously sweet hint of spice.

Wolf Blass Yellow Label: Cabernet Sauvignon. Smoky aroma, thick, fruity, spicy with hints of vanilla.

Wolf Blass Green Label: Shiraz. I would die for this and it wouldn't be a sad death. Thick, velvet fruits with glimpses of chocolate.

Wolf Blass Blue Label: Shiraz/Grenache. Lovely young wine. Clever blending of complex red fruit flavours.

Whites

Hardy's Bankside: Chardonnay. Hints of cut grass softened by mellow cream.

Hunter Ridge: Chardonnay. Creamy, oaky, with spikes of lime and finish of cut grass.

Jacob's Creek: Chardonnay. A classic of the Chardonnay era, lately underrated. Good value for a wine that uses the oak edge tastefully, never allowing it to overshadow the fruits.

Knappstein Clare Valley: Chardonnay. Now this is the perfect example of an oakiness that is held in the distance, allowing citrus and cream flavours to come through.

La Baume: Sauvignon Blanc. Easy-going with a slight tropical zing. Not the most elegant or challenging of whites, but light and fun.

Lindemans Cawarra: Chardonnay. Tropical fruits and unexpected lemon twists. Refreshing.

Lindemans Bin 65: Chardonnay. Apricots, peaches, pear ... fruit abounds in this highly refreshing and well-balanced Chardonnay.

Mirrabroo: Chardonnay. Jungle fruits kick-start a taste that finishes well with oaky aftertaste.

Oxford Landing: Chardonnay. Light, fresh, zingy, young and fun.

Oxford Landing: Limited Release Viognier. Apricot and peach.

Oxford Landing: Sauvignon. Melon and limes. All those ludicrous wine clichés, like 'cheeky little number' or 'precocious' seem to actually apply to this wine.

Penfolds Koonunga Hill: Chardonnay. A personal favourite. Good value. Pineapples and cream, topped by vanilla and strong hints of refreshing limes.

Penfolds Rawson's Retreat Bin 21: Semillon/Chardonnay.

New World

A little out of the ordinary. The citrus Semillon clashes entertainingly with vanilla Chardonnay.

Peter Lehmann: Chardonnay. Peaches and cream, but the spicy finish is unexpected and slightly unsettling.

Rosemount: Gewürtztraminer/Riesling. Incredible spiky lime and lemon flavours. Perfect as an accompaniment to spicy food. Refreshing and cool.

Rosemount Estate: Semillon. The experts suggest that this is Rosemount's finest affordable wine. Certainly unusual, with floral hints and the unexpected zing of citrus.

Tatachilla: Sauvignon Blanc/Semillon. Crisp, sharp limy flavours softened by a gentle nuttiness.

Tatachilla Breakneck Creek: Chardonnay. Lovely fresh cream overtones with tropical fruits and subtle oaky finish.

Wolf Blass: Barrel Fermented Chardonnay. Absolutely fantastic. Has the aroma, the intense fruit and the strong spicy finish one might expect from a much more expensive bottle. I can't recommend this too highly.

Woolshed: Chardonnay. Buttery overtones and hints of, honestly, cheese. Strong creamy finish.

New Zealand

Reds

CJ Pask: Cabernet Sauvignon/Merlot. Thick, red fruits balanced by unusually high acidity. Unusual and intriguing.

Coopers Creek: Cabernet Sauvignon. Strong vanilla aromas cover a heart of blackcurrant. Complex and perfectly balanced.

Cooks: Cabernet Sauvignon. Lightish and tinged with delicate flavourings. Blackcurrants are matched equally by hints of mint.

Delegat's Hawke's Bay: Cabernet Sauvignon/Merlot. Elegant and velvety, rich fruits with chocolate hints.

Esk Valley: Merlot/Cabernet Sauvignon. Black cherry and peppers feature in this well-balanced wine. The overall effect is strangely smooth.

Matheson Estate: Cabernet Sauvignon/Merlot. Incredibly smooth, rich fruits balanced by spiced oakiness.

Saints: Cabernet Sauvignon. Rich and laced with heavy chocolate and dried fruit spices. Great with any kind of cheese ... as long as it is blue.

New World

Whites

Cooks: Sauvignon Blanc. Light, fluffy, lemon meringue with gooseberry aromas. Quaintly complex.

Corbans Cottage Block: Chardonnay. Rich toffee flavours complemented by ripe autumnal fruit. More elegant than the average Chard!

Corbans Waimanu: Sauvignon Blanc. Light, floral notes fronting lemon and lime flavours. A light wine, crisp and fun.

Grove Mill: Chardonnay. Crumbly pastry aroma and a creamy fruit heart. Very unusual, and neat balance.

Judd Estate: Chardonnay. Thick, fruity aromas and vanilla oak edge. The finish is of unripe melon.

Lincoln Hawke's Bay: Sauvignon Blanc. Powerful green fruits softened by slight touches of vanilla.

Mills Reef: Sauvignon Blanc. Creamy fruit flavours which sweeten towards the finish. Clever and well-rounded.

Montana: Sauvignon Blanc. Elegant, very intense mix of green fruits – limes, gooseberries, unripe green melons and even a hint of grapefruits.

Montana: Chardonnay. Unlikely flowery notes and sweet lemons, long creamy finish. Perfectly balanced and very reasonably priced.

Oyster Bay: Sauvignon Blanc. Cut grass, lemon and limes. The aroma has a strong sting of citrus. A zesty, heady wine.

Stoneleigh: Chardonnay. Lemons, limes, melons and a rich grassy aroma all funnel down to a clever, memorable finish. Leaves a zing in the mouth.

Twin Island: Unwooded Chardonnay. Great as an alternative. Very complex with a honeysuckle nose, cut grass heart and zingy lemon finish.

Villa Maria: Chardonnay. Lightly oaked, citrus fruits and melons with a honeyed finished. Delicious.

South Africa

Reds

Bellingham: Pinotage. Tastes as if it has been made from a hedgerow. Blackberries, raspberries and fruitcake spices in the rich finish.

Drostdy-Hof: Cabernet Sauvignon. Leathery touches and velvety richness spliced by chocolate flavours and, right at the death, a hint of mint.

Drodsty-Hof: Merlot. Hearty, full-flavoured, fruity wine with soft, ripe tannins and a delicate touch of oak.

New World

Elegant rather than complex. Good value.

Drodsty-Hof: Pinotage. A spicy, sharp, precocious wine. Not exactly subtle but certainly intense.

Fairview Estate: Zinfandel/Cinsault. Like your old grandma's blackberry jam. The anarchic Zinfandel grape is allowed to run riot in this rich dark wine blessed with hints of oak.

Fairview Estate: Pinotage. Another example of dark, deep fruits with woody hints and raspberries in the heart which refuse to fade and are still evident in the otherwise spiced finish.

Groot Constantia: Pinotage. A good example of a complex wine with perfectly balanced qualities. The fruits are cleverly opposed by a wintry spiciness. Both elements still linger in the finish.

Groot Constantia: Cabernet Sauvignon. Intriguing. Strong touches of cream soften the blackcurrant and apple flavours. Tobacco on the nose.

Long Mountain: Cabernet Sauvignon. Raspberries and strawberries battle in the heart of a flavour that hardens to a slight unexpected tartness in the finish.

Oak Village: Pinotage. Earthy, dark red and deeply fruity. Not huge in length, but distinctive and flavourful.

Pinotage Impala: Look for this. Once past the harsh nose, a wonderful blackcurrant and apple flavour mix and, just as you are enjoying that, in rushes a nutty, spicy finish.

Pinnacle: Cabernet Sauvignon. Hard to find but a good wine for those who can't quite take the richness of good red wine without risking that morning headache. This is lighter, with strawberry flavourings and a delicate touch of spice at the finish.

Mount Disa: Pinotage. A dusky, intense wine, full-blooded with hints of chocolate on the nose.

Somerfield South African Pinotage: Strong, dark, handsome, full-blooded and very, very fruity. The contrasting fruit flavours linger in the length.

Whites

De Wetshof Estate: Chardonnay. Light apple and melon flavourings hardened by touches of clever spice and just a hint of vanilla.

Kumala: Semillon/Chardonnay. Very well priced for such a good blend. Apple pie and cream at the heart, followed by a hint of gooseberry that lingers at the finish.

Laborie Estate: Chardonnay. Tropical fruits bubble away

in an acidic but refreshing wine which bites entertainingly at the finish.

Plaisir de Merle: Chardonnay. Upmarket, rich and deeply wooded, yet the balance pulls the fruit back to the front in the length. A good bet for a more complex than usual Chard.

Springfield Estate: Sauvignon Blanc. Sharp, unripe gooseberries attack from the start. They don't mellow either. Zingy, refreshing finish.

Springfield Estate: Semillon. A full flush of green fruits attacks the palate at the start and the flavours intensify towards the hot, spicy finish.

Villiera Estate: Gewürztraminer. Citrus on the nose, with cut grass and melons to follow. Clever balance and strong lime and pepper finish. Complex yet good fun.

Wide River: Sauvignon Blanc. Fresh, dry, early gooseberries softened in the middle by a subtle creaminess. Neatly balanced and elegant.

North America

Reds

Beringer Vineyard: Cabernet Sauvignon. The nose is thick with ripe plums and the following taste doesn't disappoint. The fruit flavours turn dry in the finish, which is an unusual touch.

Boardwalk: Cabernet Sauvignon. Black pruney and dried fruit flavours with leathery overtones, all of which softens to a lovely flavourful finish.

Canyon Road: Cabernet Sauvignon. Sweet, strong, purple plums with cinnamon spices and rich tannins.

Fetzer: Cabernet Sauvignon. A Californian classic. The oakiness seems massive and attacks in the nose before rich plums and damsons hold the heart. A hint of mint completes the picture. Not cheap, but everyone loves it.

Fetzer, Eagle Peak: Cabernet Sauvignon. Mulberry and redcurrants flavours balanced by strong tannins.

Fetzer: Pinot Noir. One of the most expensive wines in this list, but worth it for special occasion. Flavours of beetroots (honestly) and over ripe fruits. Not fantastically complex, but absolutely perfectly balanced. Elegant and understated. Not quite the American norm.

New World

Ernest and Julio Gallo, Copperbridge: Cabernet Sauvignon. An unflashy, straight-down-the-line Cab. Blackcurrant with a touch of mint.

Garnet Point: Cabernet Sauvignon/Merlot. Sharp, precocious with a strong attack of fruits. Not exactly complex and short on length, but distinctive.

Ernest and Julio Gallo, Turning Leaf: Cabernet Sauvignon. Very rich indeed, intense blackcurrants with enormous fruity tail.

Ironstone: Cabernet Sauvignon. The fruity tones are unusually powerful here, balanced by velvet mocha flavours. Chocolate in the finish.

Sutter Home: Cabernet Sauvignon. Hedgerow flavours battle away, with blackcurrants to the fore. Touch of tobacco late in the taste. Not a long finish, but well-balanced nevertheless.

Wente: Cabernet Sauvignon. Very well-balanced wine with unlikely shards of coffee peaking through the jamlike fruits.

Whites

Bonterra Vineyards: Chardonnay. Banana at the fore, with pineapples and vanilla tones lurking with intent. Melon in the finish.

Camelot Vineyard: Chardonnay. Lemon and lime heart with pine needle nose. Refreshing and good zingy lemon finish. A bit pricey.

Dry Creek: Fumé Blanc. Very unusual. Think of asparagus tips on the nose and green fruit at the heart. The flavours linger well and turn cleverly acidic in the finish. Perfect on a hot sunny day ... or on a drab winter's day when you are dreaming of hot sunny days.

Dry Creek: Chenin Blanc. Creamy on the nose, nicely balanced with a bubbly fruit aftertaste. Good fun.

Ernest and Julio Gallo, Turning Leaf: Chardonnay. As you would expect, classier than the oaky norm, with intriguing hints of gooseberry poking through the general smoothness.

Ernest and Julio Gallo, Estate Bottled Chardonnay: The oakiness does dominate a little too much, but it's nice to taste the melon and mangoes bursting through in the heart, topped by sweet burnt orange.

Fetzer Sundial: Chardonnay. Another classic. More limy and grapefruity than you would expect, softened by rich cream and a lush honeyed finish. Not as trendy as it once was, but who cares? Still as glorious as a Malibu sunset.

Fetzer: Viognier. Petrol on the nose. Don't be put off. It helps to pull through a lovely mix of pineapples, apricots before it all folds to a spiced finish. Quite wonderful.

Montevina: Chardonnay. Softer than most. The tropical fruit flavours dip into vanilla. The overall effect is a wonderful smoothness that most people seem to love.

Sutter Home: Chardonnay. Rich melons and creamy vanilla touches. Good value and nicely balanced. No sting in the tail, but the balance continues to the end.

Stonybrook Vineyards: Chardonnay. Flowery on the nose with peppery pineapples emerging in the later taste.

South America

Chile – Reds

Tierra del Fuego: Cabernet Sauvignon. Stewed fruits soon give way to an intense invasion of sweet blackcurrants before the whole things fades slowly at the finish. Good, balanced complex Cab at a reasonable price. Remarkable quality.

Vina Carta: Cabernet Sauvignon (Antigua Reserve). Richly spiced. Dried fruits and glace cherries all thin out in an elegant finish.

Vina Carta: Merlot. Heavy plum flavours topped with

hints of spice and, at the end, a touch of mint. Very neatly rounded.

Isla Negra: Syrah. Thick with fruits and topped by peppery tones which strengthen at the finish.

Errazuriz: Cabernet Sauvignon. Has always been a favourite in this house. Intriguing, medicinal hints on the nose leads you into an intense mix of blackberries and ripe raspberries. Strong, lovely, lingering sensual finish.

Casa Leona: Cabernet Sauvignon. Herby nose with dried fruits gives way to sweet black plums and chocolate finish.

Rowan Brook: Cabernet Sauvignon. Smoked plums and dark jams, topped by blackcurrant nose.

Santa Rita: Cabernet Sauvignon. Mint on the nose ... very complex this ... brings you into a liquorice, redcurrants and blackberry heart and a slight vanilla finish.

Valdivieso: Merlot. Interesting tobacco tones on the nose dip to ripe blackcurrant heart and lush finish.

Underraga: Cabernet Sauvignon. Minty notes on the nose, with plum jam centre and soft long finish.

Underraga: Carmenère Reserve. Unusual this. Mushrooms battle with hedgerow fruits, with pine leaves lingering in the shadows.

Chile – Whites

Casa Leona: Chardonnay. Unexpected and fun. Bananas on the nose, with pineapples in the heart of the flavours, hints of oak and spices in the finish. Very good balance and price.

Tierra del Fuego: Chardonnay. A good fun white. Zingy limes balanced by enticing pears and melons. Light, dry and relatively harmless. Unlikely to give you a headache.

Cono Sur: Gewürztraminer. Most Cono Sur wines provide good quality at good value and this is one of the very best. Woody, spicy and full of lush green fruits and cut grass finish.

Isla Negra: Chardonnay. Apricots and cream, pineapples and honeydew melons all forming a lovely central battle, with spices waiting to leap in at the finish.

Rowan Brook: Chardonnay. Oranges in the undertones, citrus on the nose and a delicious buttery finish. Perfectly proportioned.

Errazuriz: Chardonnay. Strong on vanilla with pineapples and apricots bursting through. Slight woody hints and spice at the end.

Valdivieso: Chardonnay. Hearty oak with touches of Marmite, topped by zingy lemons and limes. Another unusual wine from this intriguing producer.

Argentina – Reds

Bright Brothers: Shiraz. Strawberry on the nose with richer, darker fruits lurking to give way to faint chocolate finish.

Bodegas: Shiraz. Very spicy on the nose, unexpected green fruit flavours follow and a herby twist at the end.

Etchart: Cabernet Sauvignon. Warm supple aromas guide you towards berries and spices which string out to extraordinary length.

Isla Negra: Firriato. Plummy and purple. Raspberries and black plums dominate the heart and allow faint spices in at the end. Well balanced and good value.

Isla Negra: Syrah. Deep cherry and spicy wine, topped by plummy aromas.

Rafael Estate: Tempranillo. From wandering wine-maker Hugh Ryman. Red berries on the nose with herbal red base. The oakiness is cleverly allowed to creep in towards the fruity finish.

Santa Julia: Syrah. Aromas of stewing fruits, like a grandmother's kitchen. Full cherry flavours in the heart and leathery finish.

Y2K San Juan: Shiraz. Crisp berries and eucalyptus on the nose, intense fruit heart. An unlikely combination but it certainly works.

Argentina – Whites

Alamos Ridge: Chardonnay. Limy aromas followed by a fruit bowl mixture, cleverly held in place by good acidity. Finishes well, leaving melon on the tongue.

Argento: Chardonnay. Has been picking up good reviews of late. Low in price. Not particularly complex but does have a certain delicate limy elegance. Traces of vanilla towards the end.

Santa Julia: Chardonnay. The oakiness has a different twist. Like burning vanilla essence with touches of pine kernels.

Europe

Italy

Reds

Cabernet Sauvignon Merlot Basilicata: A classic Italian red. Powerful, alluring aromas lead to deep, hearty fruit and strong dark chocolate to finish. Great.

Canaletto Primitivo Di Puglia: Intense, complex, plummy red, heavy on tobacco and leather. Intense powerful finish.

Capitel San Rocco Ripasso: Valpolicella, but produced in the traditional manner. The cherry base holds rich chocolate and spicy flavourings which spill out to a vast finish. Stylish and elegant, the Italian way.

Clemente V11: Chianti Classico. Strong cherries on the nose with rich sweet young fruits popping to the surface. Fantastic value. Good crisp tobacco finish, too.

Conti Serristori: Chianti Classico. Fruit cake and cherries giving way to lush berries and rich strong tannins in the finish.

Massovecchio: Chianto Classico. More expensive but worth splashing out on simply for the blend of dark cherry fruits and rich Italian coffee. The finish is long and sensual.

Europe

Merlot Trentino: Mulberry flavours balanced by warming woodiness with hints of spice and nutty finish. It's a complex rout but this wine gets there in entertaining fashion, and with considerable style.

Nero di Avola: Unusual Sicilian wine where medicinal tones lead you to a soft, lush fruity heart and cleverly balanced oaky finish.

Pinot Nero Fruivini: Pinot Noir. Very much a classic. Good lashings of stewed fruits and earthy tones leading to rich fruit finish.

Valpolicella Classico Superiore Grola Ottomarzo: Spicy nose and deep, deep, cherry flavourings leading to vanilla finish.

Valpolicella Classico Superiore Zenato: Damsons on the nose balanced by green bitter tannins.

Valpolicella Ripasso: Sunny, warming fruits ... Italy in a bottle! Ripe red fruits and smoky aromas.

Valpolicella Classico dei Nicalo: A perfect example of how Valpolicella doesn't have to cost the earth to attain complexity. Here is a bitter black cherry aroma topping a nutty, full-blooded and savoury wine with elegant length.

Germany

Whites

Bernkasteler Badstube: Riesling. Incredibly cheap for a glorious golden wine simply dripping with honeyed flavourings. Fresh and sweet to the finish.

Bernkasteler Badstube: Riesling Kabinett. Flinty, grapefruit flavours lead into a herbaceous mix of floral flavours, Finishes softly. If there is a such thing as a feminine German wine, this is it.

Graacher Himmelreich: Riesling. Sweet wine, a full flush of rosés and citrus flavours which sharpens to tart green apples at the finish.

Grans Fassian: Riesling. Extremely complex. Stony hints give way to pineapples and lemons with long honeyed finish.

Kenderman Northern Star: Riesling. Apricots and pineapples to the fore. Hardens a little late in the taste. Finishes in fizzy acidity.

Niersteiner Oelberg: Riesling. Flowers on the nose, sharpened by hints of petrol. Highly refreshing and delicate wine which fades elegantly to a fruity finish.

Piesporter Goldtröpfchen: Riesling Kabinett. Sweet and cool, autumnal flavours, nuts and pine with lime zing towards the finish.

Schloss Schönborn: Riesling. Sweet, honey on the nose. Quaint mix of soft fruits to follow, all softened further by buttery finished. Unexpected and rather good.

Urziger Wurzgarten: Reisling Kabinett. Delicious ripe apple flavours with lovely lime fresh acidity at the finish.

Zeltinger Himmelreich: Riesling Kabinett. Strong limes to the fore, spiciness complements the citrus flavours later in the taste.

Zimmermann Graeff: Liebfraumilch. This outstanding wine firmly kicks away the old notion of dull Liebfraumilch. Hints of peach at the heart. Honey and butter to the finish.

Austria

Whites

Samling 88: Trockenbeerenauslese. At the top end of our range, but probably worth it, if the occasion demands, as it is like wandering into a flower shop, aromas everywhere, battling for dominance as the wine settles with a smooth, velvety heart. Sweet and lovely.

Weingut Dolle. 'Oscar': Chardonnay. Weird but good balance. Salty notes may remind you of seaside holidays while the green fruits carry the taste through to a curiously dry finish.

Welschriesling Bouvier: Trockenbeerenauslese. Absolutely perfect balance, with honey and lemons held in place by strong tar-like aromas and strong peppery finish.

Spain

Reds

Bach: Merlot. Flowers and mint. A curious combination, but they hit you from the nose. The flavours are dark, though. Burnt blackberries and caramel.

Baron de Ley: Rioja. Strong, stout, vast mess of fruit with hints of nettles and tobacco towards the dense finish.

Berberana Dragon: Tempranillo. Strawberries and vanilla. Oaky at the heart and strong rich finish.

Castillo Labastida: Rioja. Oaky Rioja softened by plums and custard flavours and gorgeous berries towards the finish.

Castillo de Liria: Tempranillo. Definitely worth looking out for. The wine has none of the harsh, faintly vinegar flavours that you might expect from a cheap Spanish red. Instead you will find a lush, soft fruity wine with light tannins and a deliciously delicate finish.

Espiral: Tempranillo. Once providers of dull, typical 1970s Spanish plonks, now rising to a rich and juicy perfection.

Gandia: Cabernet Sauvignon. Comparatively light red wine where the blackcurrant aromas are balanced by late-harvest redcurrants and raspberries.

Marqués De Griñon: Rioja. Unusual dusty aromas give the wine an enigmatic quality. The flavours are suitably rich and deep. Dry fruits towards the finish.

Marqués de Riscal: Tempranillo. Full-blooded red. Strong structure and a good alternative to Rioja. Massed fruits on the finish.

Navajas Tinto Crianza: Lovely plummy wine, balanced with soft fruits and just a hint of vanilla.

Sierra Alta: Cabernet Sauvignon. Incredible looking wine. Don't be put off by the fact that it is bright purple! It tastes much better than it looks. The expected blackcurrants are there but are firmly held in place by lighter fruits, raspberries and even hints of strawberry.

Torres Sangre de Toro: Cabernet Sauvignon. Hedgerow fruits battle away spikily, with hints of milky coffee towards the finish.

Viña Diezma: Rioja. Burning damsons and stewing plums with hints of chocolate towards the finish.

France

Alsace – White

Domaine Mittnacht-Klack: Gewürtztraminer. *On Golden Pond* in a bottle. As autumnal as a wine can be. Warm, sunny heart, full of spice and delicate ripe fruits punching through towards the end.

Schlumberger: Riesling. Unusually flowery nose which makes the juicy fruit heart seem almost shocking.

Toka: Pinot Gris. Deep, dark, over-ripe peaches with touches of cinnamon and long creamy finish.

Beaujolais – Red

Beaujolais Villages – Domaine de Bacarra: Cabernet Sauvignon. Incredible, sweet caramel on the nose with a crisp red apples and honey heart, followed by enormous, sumptuous fruity length.

Fleurie Georges Duboeuf: A favourite around here. All manner of berry fruit bursting through to meet a lovely warming finish.

Morgon Cave Boccabarteille: Cabernet Sauvignon. Thick, almost purple wine with raspberry overtones and velvet, jammy heart. Perfect balance.

Morgon Georges Duboeuf: Cabernet Sauvignon. Young, fun and frolicsome. Cherries matched with plums, strawberries towards the finish.

Bordeaux – Red

Baron Philippe de Rothschild: Médoc. Currants, red and black, melt together on the nose while vanilla flavours ease through the fruity heart.

Calvet Reserve: Claret. Up the market, slightly, this is two-thirds Merlot and one-third Cabernet Sauvignon and the balance is just about right. Tinges of dark French oak, like smelling a highly polished sideboard. Good finish too.

Calvet Cuvée: Claret. Very, very cheap. Not as complex as more expensive Clarets, but a decent alternative to New World reds. The up-front blackberries are pleasing, especially as they melt into soft caramel.

Cave Co-op de St Emilion: Just a complex, soft, accessible, relaxed, easy-going little Claret. Is there a better wine in the world to enjoy with strong cheese than a good but mid-priced Claret? Answer? No.

Château Grand Tuillac. Côtes de Castillon: Mellow spices, warm blackberry fruits all melting to a perfect roundness. Exquisite finish.

Château Guerin Bellevue: Cabernet Sauvignon. Plummy wine with shards of vanilla. From the Yvon Mau stable. Clever and perfect with a good French brie.

Château L'Abbaye de St-Ferme: Bordeaux Superiore. This is another French wine that is built to take on the New World. Nothing old fashioned about this. The concentration of spices is way beyond anything that Australia might offer and, just at the finish and in the nick of time- in comes a rush of vibrant fruit.

Château la Perrière: Cabernet Sauvignon. Strawberry flavours hiding beneath spicy nose and chocolate hints in the finish.

Yvon Mau: Saint Emilion. Intriguing and clever balance. Slightly more acidity than you might expect, countered by strong, vibrant fruits.

Yvon Mau Mauregard: Cabernet Sauvignon. Strong blackcurrants and bramble fruits, spiced by hints of nettles. Lighter towards the finish.

Bordeaux – White

Château Filhot: Sauternes. Classic sweet white, indicative of warm, humid summer days. The flavour concentration is so complex I could fill the page with description alone. A bouquet of flowers dipped in a vat of honey and allowed to dry out in the midday sun.

Rivers Meet: Sauvignon Blanc. Flinty heart and smoky on the nose. Underneath lies a buttery heart which hardens to fruits towards the finish.

Yvon Mau: Graves Blanc. Early gooseberry flavours beneath floral nose. Vanilla tinges towards the sweeter finish.

Burgundy – Red

Cave Co-op Buxy. Bourgogne: Pinot Noir. Jam packed with crushed strawberry fruits. Rounded structure with moderate tannins.

Chore-lès-Beaune. Bouchard Pere et Fils: Delicious, soft cherry and strawberry flavours which also hang over in the aroma. Custardy finish.

Domaine Haute Côtes de Nuits: The fruits are young, crisp green apples, hard pears, young plums all fall into place before light chocolate hints carry through to the finish.

Louis Latour, Bourgogne: Pinot Noir. Sink into soft, ripe raspberries and lumps of plums. Softened further by edges of chocolate.

Maranges Premier Cru. Joseph Drouhin: Rich cherries and

lovely strong vanilla give the nose a powerful character
while the rich jammy fruits are allowed to follow.

Burgundy – White

Bourgogne Tête de Cuvée: Chardonnay. Melon and
gooseberries dominate this unusually tart Chardonnay
which finishes like a bowl of green apple peelings.

Cave Co-op Buxy. Bourgogne Blanc: A lovely cheap but
classic white wine. Lively, zingy, fresh and highly
precocious. Elegance for everyone.

Chablis Vau Corsieres: Classic bone dry wine, crisp sharp
fruits. Hard green apples, touches of lime, hints of
melon, zings to the finish. For Chablis, should be
exceptionally cheap, too.

Chablis Premier Cru. Vielles Vignes: Steely dry with
complex depth and heady battle of lemons and
grapefruits to the fore. Perfect Chablis. Top of our price
range, though.

Mâcon-Lugny. Louis Latour: Sophisticated white Burgundy
with buttery character, lemon aromas and creamy oak to
the finish.

Loire – Red

Anjou-Villages Domaine de la Motte: A harsh, stony dryness on the nose followed by fruit bowl mixture and stewed fruit finish.

La Chapelle de Cray: Soft fruit nose with touch of sweetness. Like an old bag of sweets that has been sitting in a drawer for ten years. Nice balance and strong finish.

Sancerre Rouge. Fournier: Thick, dark velvet wine with dark chocolate aromas and spices to the finish.

Loire – White

Argilo Vouvray sec. Domaine Bourillon d'Orleans: A complex, bone dry Vouvray with sharp, tingly finish. The spirit of the Loire.

Muscadet Sur Lie. Château la Touche: Look for this. Its fantastic low price often tends to put people off. They don't know what they are missing. Spritzy, yeasty, full taste with vanilla tinges.

Reuilly. Henri Beurdin: This is a perfect Loire Sauvignon, full of fresh fruit with a clean crisp finish.

Sancerre. Roger Neveu: Ripe rhubarb and gooseberry fruit with zesty mineral texture. Delicate balance and finish.

Sancerre La Chaudouillonne: Whole mess of mineral freshness balanced by strong citrus fruits. Again, an incredibly elegant, beautifully proportioned white.

Rhône – Red

Châteauneuf-du-Pape Château Simian: A cheaper 'Pape' and well worth looking out for. Strong purplish colour and hearty, fruity wine with powerful pepper finish.

Côtes du Rhône Les Chevaliers aux Lys d'Or: Grenache, Syrah, Carignan and Cinsault all mix in this unbelievably cheap, gentle wine. Light rather than complex, but blessed with a decent finish.

Côtes du Rhône Guigal: Another big grape mix producing a complex plummy wine with slight touches of apricots.

Côtes du Luberon Château Val Joanis. A red wine with great subtle qualities...unusual in itself. There is a sense of elegance to this wine that is rare in any Rhône red, let alone on that is mid- to low-priced.

Domaine St Anne Cuvée Notre-Dame: A spiced, peppered nose and blackberry jam heart. Great strong winterish wine with huge finish.

Lirac Les Esperelles: Well rounded, supple red. Cherries fighting with blackcurrants and powerful finish.

South-West France – Red

Merlot VDP de Côtes de Gascogne: Wow! Bubbly plum jam. Hints of sweetness and raspberries in the finish.

Château la Jaubertie: Cabernet Sauvignon. Smoky enticing nose, deep fruit heart. Almost in Bordeaux, almost a Claret and a superb alternative.

South-West France –White

Domaine du Tariquet: Sauvignon Blanc. Forgive me for mentioning this exquisite little mid-priced wine...again. With pineapple around the edges and tropical fruit heart, it always seemed to be the most elegant and sophisticated white wine in its price range. Hunt it down.

Les Jardins du Bouscasse: Lovely ripe melons attacked at the edges by gooseberries and grapefruits...oh and strong grassy finish.

Conclusion

And so we finish this minute list – more of a guide really – in the South of France. Where better? Well, in terms of wine, there are a number of better regions just to the north on the map, just before on the list. For lesser countries, for Mexico – La Cetto, remember? – there seemed little point in repeating the wines mentioned earlier. As to France, Italy, Germany, Australia etc... this book is just dipping a toe, a 'tasting', if you like.

Are you still confused? Well, probably. But at least, now, when you stagger around that supermarket, a few countries, a few producers, a few grapes...a few words may just leap from the bottle and tempt you towards trying something new.

And that, really, is the main point. While you should never, ever lose sight of French wines – such a thing would be unforgivable – and you should return there every four bottles or so, as the quality of wine across the world continues to get better and better...and better, then what fun to experiment! Slovenian wine? Go for it. Brazilian wine? Well...yes, maybe, although you'd be far better with an Argentinean or Chilean Cab. But then again, a whole

Conclusion

new batch of Brazilian imports may come in and prove me wrong!

Listen to the experts but don't take them too seriously. Don't mock that Lambrusco Bianco-drinking couple. Offer them a glass of Wolf Blass and, if they turn their noses up at that, let them be happy in their ignorance. It doesn't really matter. It really doesn't. Wine is a side issue.

Who am I kidding? It's a passion. There is nothing in the world quite like wine. It is endlessly fascinating.

For proof, think of the best meal in the world. This meal doesn't take place in some fancy restaurant. No. It is out in the open, on a hillside in the sun. It could be anywhere warm on earth. The food is simple, incredibly simple. It is a picnic. You crack open a bread roll with your hands. Place a slice of your favourite cheese on it. Savour the flavour, soak in the heat, make light talk with your partner, pour the red wine and just sit back and enjoy! That's all you need. Enjoy that experience fully and you are a gastronome.

And just think how empty that wonderful experience would be without its most glorious and magic component … the glass of wine!

FREQUENTLY

ASKED

QUESTIONS

ABOUT

WINE

Frequently Asked Questions About Wine

Although wine sophistication is increasing, for all of us it seems, day by day...there are still a number of basic wine questions that seem to stump people. Now, I have to say, fear not. If you don't know what tannins are, it doesn't matter. If you don't know what an appellation is, well, so what? It does not make you a social inadequate. In fact, there are certain circumstances where the reverse is the case. Then again, perhaps these are things that you might like to know. Read on:

Should I have white wine with fish and red wine with meat?

No. Here is a fact. Most of the wine that you can buy today will go with most of the food you are ever likely to prepare.

The only problem occurs when certain foods clash horribly with certain wines. The good news is that this is very rare. The bad news is that it is really something that you simply have to discover for yourself. Now, that might sound like a cop out, but it isn't. People are different. They have different tastes. You have to find your own likes and dislikes.

As to not having red wine with fish, this is complete and utter rubbish. There are many parts of, say, Europe – Portugal for instance – that are world famous for producing red wines that are perfectly matched for the local fish dishes. I don't believe there is a single person on earth capable of convincing me that, say, a Dover Sole dish isn't the perfect companion for a good Beaujolais.

Obviously certain wines do complement certain foods. Anyone who has nibbled on blue Stilton while drinking a lovely Cabernet Sauvignon knows that! Also, sweet dessert wines are simply perfect with, well, with sweet desserts! A crisp, dressed salad will be perfectly matched with a Sauvignon Blanc. These may seem obvious examples and that is because there really are no rules at all. And if there are – break them! I personally feel that a bottle of cold lager all but ruins a good curry. Not everyone would agree but, if you are a curry and lager devotee, just once try your Rogan Josh with a powerful red wine and a bottle of water. Fantastic.

What is acidity?

It isn't a good word, really, is it? A bottle that is said to have 'high acidity' might well put off a non wine lover. Well, it shouldn't. Acidity works on a number of levels. It is a good preservative. It also lifts the flavours from the main body of the wine. It is also a myth that acidity levels soften as a wine ages. They don't and they don't need to. High acidity can be a bad thing, as in a cheap red that is way past its peak. Acidity is

Frequently Asked Questions About Wine

really a question of balance. High acidity works well in some wines but not in others.

What are tannins?

Tannins are a group of organic chemicals found in the bark of trees and in some fruits. As far as wine is concerned, they can be found in grapes, in the seeds and skin in particular. Here comes the complex bit. The tannins in the seeds can be particularly bitter. (If you bite on a grape seed and experience that sharp woody taste, that's the tannin.) The desirable tannins come from the skins. You will taste them, most obviously, in older style wines. French reds, in particular. They add body and character to the wine. But, once again, it's all a question of balance.

Should I open red wine an hour before serving to 'let it breathe'? And should I decant red wine?

OK, once and for all, uncorking a wine to 'let it breathe' has absolutely no effect whatsoever. The idea is to allow air to get to the wine. Well, it can't, can it? Simply because of the wine bottle's neck. Only the top half-inch of wine could possibly be affected. The only way to let air to a wine is to decant. However, with nearly all the wines you buy today, this isn't necessary at all. If you have an aged, slightly musty wine then, yes, it might well benefit from exposure. But even then, if you swirl the wine around your glass before drinking, the effect will be so much the better. A decanter might look posh, though.

Wine glasses – big or little?

They should be big enough to hold a decent amount and yet still have room to swirl. Simple as that. Try to avoid trendy coloured glasses. You need to see the colour, that is part of the experience.

Does all wine improve with age?

No it doesn't. Some does. A deep, complex and probably expensive red may soften to perfection over the years. Serious wine drinkers, buyers and collectors will lay down wines for investment purposes and, occasionally, the quality will improve along with the price. But the important point is that, for the average wine drinker, there really isn't any point in worrying about this any more. Today's wines are better, cheaper and more reliable than ever before. The world of wine is in your corner shop. With so much to explore – more and more every week – is there really any point in allowing wines

Frequently Asked Questions About Wine

to age? Some would say yes. Some would vigorously argue the point. Personally, I think that life is too short.

What does 'Appellation Controllée' mean?

The best quality of French wine. A general quality level that takes into account soil, grape, varieties, levels of alcohol and even the way that vineyards and cellars are run. Attaining 'Appellation Controllée' will lift a wine and a vineyard on to a higher level.

What does 'Vin de Pays' mean?

A straight translation would be 'Country wine'. What it actually refers to is a wine that is better than the basic table wine, or Vin de Table.